Derby
Memories

Anton Rippon

NORTH BRIDGE PUBLISHING

First published in Great Britain in 2013 by
North Bridge Publishing
20 Chain Lane
Mickleover
Derby DE3 9AJ

ISBN 978-0-9926779-1-6

Book design by Graham Hales, Derby

Printed and bound by Berforts Information Press Ltd

Contents

Introduction

THE OLDER you become, the more you value the past. As the years roll on and you enter what some describe as the "autumn years" of your life – a description I always find disquieting – the more you want to look back. It starts the day you suddenly hear yourself saying: "I remember when it was all fields around here." That is when you realise that you are turning into your parents.

For those of us who grew up in Derby in the years after the Second World War – and, if truth were told, right into the 1970s – the city we see today has changed so much from the town we first remember. Some things are better. Some things are worse. When things are worse they generally revolve around people's behaviour. We can recall a time when it would have been unthinkable to hear men swearing openly in front of women on a bus. Nowadays you hear even teenagers of both sexes doing just that. We remember when children were in awe of their local bobby. When you could walk back from the Midland railway station in the early hours of the morning and feel quite safe. Nobody was going to mug you. We remember a time when you really could leave your front door off the latch while you nipped to the corner shop. And recalling all this isn't the result of looking back through the rose-tinted lenses of distant memory. It really was like that. No wonder we like to look back.

Few of us are comfortable with unfamiliarity. A friend of mine summed it up beautifully when he said: "It's just that I like things the way they used to be." If we were fortunate to enjoy a reasonable childhood, at least one free from poverty and hunger, then I suppose most of us would agree. We like to look back to a gentler time, when it was safe to roam abroad during those long summer school holidays, when going out on a Saturday night meant no more than joining a long queue for the pictures, or a quiet pint in a city centre pub, and making sure that you were on the last bus before the inspector blew his whistle. It was a safer, much less vulgar world.

And that is pretty much what this book is about – looking back.

I've brought together what I hope will be a gentle ramble down memory lane, mixing my own meanderings with some of those who I have had the pleasure of interviewing these past 40 years, and with more recent contributions from Derbeians, and former Derbeians, who retain a fondness for this place we call home. I hope that you enjoy it and that it may evoke a few pleasant memories of your own.

Anton Rippon
Derby
2013

Gerard Street Memories

S O, THE last protests were brushed aside, the bulldozers moved in – and the final stage of Derby's inner ring road finally and forever changed the area in which I grew up. Gerard Street was cut in two, the lower half of Wilson Street all but disappeared and with it went a large swathe of the place where I was born and spent my childhood.

Yet, even after all this, it was still possible to stroll down that particular stretch of memory lane and recall the people who once made it such a wonderful place to live.

In the 21st century, it is not uncommon to live in a house for years and still know very little about even your closest neighbours. Yet when I was growing up, I knew practically everyone in Gerard Street, even though it was half a mile long. Most of all, I knew the other kids.

My two best friends were John Burns and Colin Shaw. John lived at 16 Webster Street, the little road on whose corner sat our house. I spent a lot of time at number 16. At four years my senior, I regarded John as an older brother, and his mum and my mum were also friends.

Colin Shaw lived at 142 Gerard Street with his parents, Arthur and Dolly. I also spent a lot of time there, playing Subbuteo tabletop football; we had a proper league and even "floodlit" matches, contrived by switching off the room lights and illuminating the pitch with four bike lamps balanced on piles of books. The most wonderful part of the Shaws' house, however, was Arthur's garden shed, which had started life as an Anderson air raid shelter. For two young lads with a vivid imagination, this became the cockpit of a Lancaster bomber on a dangerous mission over Berlin, the hull of a submarine searching for German shipping in the North Atlantic, a machine-gun emplacement in the Western Desert. We spent hundreds of hours in that shed, fighting the Second World War all over again. And the Korean War as well because, for some of the time, Colin's older brother, John, was serving as a National Serviceman in that conflict.

Our happy gang was complemented by several girls: Kathleen Radford, whose father, Cyril, was one of the local window cleaners (George Manning was the other), was a regular, as were Janet Foster, who lived in Webster Street, and Margaret Helliwell, who lived opposite us on the other side of the entry to Mick and Ivy Betts. Margaret's father, Fred, was a bit of a card. Every evening at 7.30pm prompt, Fred would emerge from his house and, looking most reluctant, stroll off to the Durham Ox, a large white-tiled 19th-century pub that stood in the corner of Gerard Street and Burton Road. Fred always had this "oh well, I suppose I must" manner when he set off the "DO", as everyone called it.

Colin Shaw's mum, Dolly, and his aunt, pictured in front of Arthur Shaw's shed that became anything two boys with vivid imaginations wanted it to be.

As he crossed the road by our house, he'd wink and ask: "Are you coming for one, then?" The funny thing was, he never asked me once I'd turned 18.

Sandra Attenborough, who lived just up the road, and Susan and Pat Mellor, a few doors further along still, also joined in our games, while Doris Wass, who lived with her family at the first house in

Webster Street, and me were the only kids in the neighbourhood to pass our 11-plus exam. I went to Bemrose School, Doris to Homelands. In the mid-1950s, the Poples came to live in Webster Street, opposite Doris. Tom Pople and his two sons, Brian and Eric, worked on the roads. Every night they'd come trudging up Gerard Street after a day's graft; Tom was a hard taskmaster who didn't let anyone off lightly, even his sons. He was also quite a comic with a dry sense of humour and the Poples soon fitted into the neighbourhood. They had two daughters: Eileen – who would one day marry my pal John Burns – and Janet.

Corner shops were the life-blood of the community. Apart from Violet Craven's little operation, which stood on the opposite side of Webster Street to our house, and which I think was more of a hobby than an income (her husband, Ernie, worked at Rolls-Royce), we mostly used a grocer's that stood on the corner of Gerard Street and Grey Street.

Over the years it had a number of owners. Eric Addelsee and his wife ran it in the early 1950s. They had a daughter, Marie, who was five years older than me and became lumbered with taking me to the Saturday children's picture show at the Alexandra cinema on Normanton Road.

The top end of Gerard Street pictured around the beginning of the 20th century. It looked much the same when I was growing up there in the late 1940s and early 1950s, apart from the fashions of course.

The Addelsees left to run a shop at Sunnyhill and their place was taken by a Mrs Harrison and her daughter and son-in-law. Mrs Harrison was an attractive unattached woman who soon gained an admirer, a former Italian prisoner-of-war called Alberto, who lived in Harcourt Street. Alberto, who sported a thin moustache which he kept jet black with some kind of dye, and who absolutely reeked of garlic, unsuccessfully wooed Mrs Harrison from the day she arrived in Gerard Street until the day she left. He also could never quite get my name right and would scurry past me, booming out: "'Ello, Tony!" as he went.

Ken Tipping and his wife, and then Owen Hobday and his wife, followed Mrs Harrison. They were all good people, always ready to give someone a lift in an emergency, or offer the use their telephone, for few households boasted one. Harry Wallis ran on off-licence on the opposite corner of Grey Street. Every Monday evening, Harry, a large red-faced man, could be seen striding up Harcourt Street, trilby hat set at a jaunty angle, on his way to the second house at the Hippodrome theatre. The Marquis of Granby pub sat next to Becket School, which I attended from 1950 to 1956. On summer evenings, Ernie Craven would stroll down to the Marquis and fill up a big white enamel jug with draught bitter before carefully returning up the street for a night by the wireless with Violet.

The Walleys of Rosengrave Street

Everyone knew the Walleys, not least because there were so many of them. Jenny Walley (now Jenny Jukes) recalled those days: "I'm the youngest of 14 children – sadly, there are only 10 us now – and I think we were possibly one of the largest families in Derby then. I grew up in a terraced house in Rosengrave Street, off Gerard Street. It was a bit like Coronation Street. Everyone knew everyone. And everybody helped each other out when needed, even to laying out the dead. They did everything for each other.

There used to be a very high wall at the top of Rosengrave Street, which made it a cul-de-sac, but that came down when they built a new estate that replaced the narrow streets known as 'the Little City' that had been there since the early 1800s. On a Saturday night my mum, who was Mrs Walley, my Aunty Gladys from Gerard Street, and a friend called Mrs Hanley (she lived in Boyer Street) all used to sit in the 'snug' at the Marquis of Granby on Gerard Street, You could just about fit the three of them in that snug; it was like Minnie, Martha and Ena from *Coronation Street*; I could have written the script. The men were all in the bar and I used to wait outside because children weren't allowed in the pub in those days – pity that law hasn't remained – and I used to get a bag of crisps and a bottle of dandelion and burdock – pure heaven. I'd sit outside the snug, on the step, especially if it was a warm night.

"Mrs Hanley's birthday was the same date as mine, and on that day every year Mum used to send me down with two cigarettes (in one of those cone-shaped sweet paper bags) for Mrs Hanley and she used to give me a half-crown. God, was I rich! I used to take newspapers, or sometimes rags, to a place in Boyer Street because they used to pay you for them; and I took empty bottles back to the off-licence, which raised a few more coppers.

"My Aunty Ivy – she was my cousin really, but you always called people aunty or uncle if you were a youngster; it was respectful and you never called adults by their first name – lived at the top of Gerard Street. They had a bathroom and I used to go there on a Friday night for my weekly bath, and when I came downstairs and sat in front of their fire, Aunty Ivy always used to give me a hot drink and Morning Coffee biscuits. Again, it was a real treat.

"Me, Mum, and Mrs Drain and her daughter, Alex, who lived in Gerard Street, used to go to the pictures on a Thursday night, to the Regal in East Street. Also, whenever I went round to play with Alex, they always had Weetabix on the breakfast table. We only had porridge at home because it went a long way, and 'stuck to your insides' as Mum used to say. I vowed that, when I grew up, I would buy Weetabix for myself, and I did. I went to Christ Church School on Normanton Road, as I think most of us did right from nursery, but it closed when I was 10, and I did my last year at Gerard Street School, where Mum cleaned. I passed my 11-plus exam and Mum gave me sixpence for passing it. Happy days … "

The Night the Hippodrome Girls Moved!

MY PAL Roger was a bright little lad. It was the early 1950s and, most afternoons, we walked home together from Becket School in Gerard Street. We'd dawdle outside our house on the corner of Webster Street, finishing off whatever conversation we'd started as we'd left the school gates. Then I'd go in for my tea, while Roger would continue to his house in Swinburne Street. One afternoon, Roger sprang a surprise: he was leaving our school at the end of that week. So, on the Friday afternoon, when we reached our house, I extended a hand: "Well, we'd better say goodbye, then."

"No," said Roger – we were all of nine years old – "Let's just say 'au revoir'". When I got in, I asked my mother what that meant (he was much worldlier than me, was Roger).

"It's French," she said, mildly irritated that I'd interrupted Mrs Dale's Diary on the wireless.

"Well, what does it mean?" I asked again.

"It means that you're saying goodbye until you meet again," she said, before returning to Mary, who was worried about Jim. "But I'm not meeting him again," I said, now more to myself because she'd reabsorbed herself in the goings on at Virginia Lodge, where Sally had apparently arrived to take Mrs Freeman to the shops. Anyway, I didn't see Roger again. And I felt rather sad about that. For about a week, anyway. Then, like most nine-year-olds, I moved on. Over the years, though, I would occasionally wonder what had become of my pal. Fifty-six years later, I had the answer: quite a lot. An email pinged on to my computer screen. Subject "When we were kids," it read simply: "I used to walk home from school, up Gerard Street, with you … Funny old world." It was from Roger Walker, the little lad I'd last seen more than half a century ago. As it turned out, I'd seen him quite a few times in the intervening years. I just didn't know it. You see Roger became an actor, one of those faces that often pop up in an episode of *The Bill*, *Emmerdale* or *EastEnders*. He's been on the cinema screen, too, not least in the 2008 film, *Brideshead Revisited*. He now lived in London, but once we'd made contact he came up to Derby for a gathering of former pupils of Becket Junior School. Like all of us, he'd changed a bit since 1954. But now I did recognise the small boy who trudged up Gerard Street with me all those years ago. It was an emotional moment.

Roger had plenty of stories to tell. I'll let him relate this one in his own words: "Here's a story that I often tell over a couple of pints, particularly to some of my actor mates. I call it: "Tonight The Girls Move.""

"My stepfather was George Walker, late of Swinburne Street, just off Burton Road. He taught violin at our house and he played violin professionally at venues in and around Derby. One of his regular engagements was playing in the pit orchestra at the Derby Hippodrome on Green Lane. This was a regular gig and he did it for a number of years in the 1950s.

"As a young lad I saw most of the shows there – pantomimes, variety shows, operas, once a circus, and even a West End play that was there on tour. With the coming of television, theatre generally went into decline and in order to put bums on seats, they started putting on nude shows at the Hippodrome. "Girlie Revues" they called them.

"Now the trouble was that the Lord Chamberlain, guardian of the country's moral sensibilities at that time, had decreed that the girls were not allowed to move. They had to pose in a static position. Indeed it was thought that the sight of a naked and gently swaying female bosom would be far too arousing for English audiences in those innocent 1950s.

"Anyway, toward the end of the revue evening the compere would come to the centre of the stage and say something like 'And now, ladies and gentlemen, for your delight we have Queen Nefertiti and her handmaidens brought here from distant Egypt!' – well, you get the picture.

"Up would go the main curtain to reveal the stage, almost in blackout, then the lights would slowly come up, the band would start playing something vaguely foreign and mysterious to reveal, behind a gauze cloth, the girls themselves. They would often be draped over articles of furniture, posed either in small groups or singly and, of course, very scantily clad. You could see their long legs and their bums, covered by brief shorts, but never a nipple. Oh no. These were covered with a sequin or a small glittery star, which had been stuck on to hide the offending part. There they would stand for a short while, then the lights would fade slowly and during a short blackout, they'd change position into another posed and static tableau then up would come the lights again … and so on.

"Anyway, one Monday in or around 1956 (I was 12) the notices appeared outside the Hippodrome: 'TONIGHT THE GIRLS MOVE.'

"Because I was George Walker's stepson, I was a regular face at the Hippodrome, both backstage and front of house (my mum, Miriam, sometimes played in the orchestra too, but not this night). So in I went and made my way upstairs to the 'Gods', the upper circle to watch the fun.

"It was really hot up there. They used carbon- arc spotlights that smoked and fumed and crackled and gave off an intense heat. Remember too, that in those days, almost everybody smoked and the cigarette and pipe smoke made for an amazing atmosphere while a packed house waited for the moment to come when the girls would move.

"Eventually after the singer, the comic, the harmonica player, the roller-skating dancers and the conjurer, the time finally arrived. The compere did his usual spiel but added ' … and yes, ladies and gentlemen, tonight, the girls will move.'

"There was a hushed anticipation. This is the moment the audience had been waiting for … it was really about to happen. The curtain rose and there, behind the gauze, stood the girls, posed as usual. The lights came up and the music swelled and then the whole centre of the stage slowly began to revolve, with the girls holding their positions. Static and frozen. Round and around they trundled, moving, yet not moving. We'd been had! What a swizz!

"Well, when the audience realised what was going on, there was uproar. Fag packets and small coins were thrown on to the stage and the orchestra was drowned out by the noise. The curtain closed to the booing sound of disappointed men. Oh, I did laugh. It was truly, the funniest thing I had seen in my young life and although I was only 12 years old, I can still say, with my hand on my heart, in all honesty, I was indeed at the Derby Hippodrome the night the girls moved."

From Burton Road to Dr Who

Back in 1964, it was. I met a young actor called Bernard Holley. Bernard was in rep at Derby Playhouse, when that theatre was in Sacheverel Street. Bernard and his wife, Jean, lived on Burton Road, just around the corner from where I lived in Gerard Street. We sometimes bumped into each other on Sunday lunchtimes in the Durham Ox, then run by Joe Kent.

Actually, something – albeit quite trivial – is bugging me here: I can't remember if that was when, just opposite the pub, butcher Ted Barker still spluttered cigarette ash over Sunday joints; or whether it was after his place had become a chip shop which, last time I passed, was still doing a roaring trade after being highly nominated by visitors to the *Derby Telegraph's* website. Anyway, never mind fish and chips, for the moment at least. The future Mrs R and me were great theatregoers in the days when – funny what you remember – before every performance at Sacheverel Street they played Kenny Ball's *The Green Leaves Of Summer*. Bernard was one of our favourite actors and recently our paths (Bernard's and mine that is; I bump into Mrs R quite regularly) crossed again.

After Derby, he moved on to greater things in theatre, film and television. Especially television: *Z-Cars* (remember PC Newcombe?), *Dr Who*, *The Bill*, *Holby City*, *Doctors*, *A Touch Of*

Frost – he's done them all and a lot more. And he is still working. Bernard fondly remembers in Derby, even if it was almost half a century ago: "My year at Derby was invaluable to me as an actor because of the variety of plays we did and parts we played. Young actors don't have that 'rep' training any more, sad to say. I kept in touch with Ian Cooper, Mary Laine and Michael Hall from the Playhouse – all sadly now deceased – with Michael being the last to go, at 93, a few years back.

"I've been one of the lucky ones – always worked in one field or another, and always earned a living – not a bad boast for an actor. What's more, I've been married to Jean – we were wed just before I started my year at Derby – for nearly 50 years, and we've lived in the same house in London for over 40."

I loved the old Playhouse, with the resident company constantly turning their hand to different parts. Performing this week's play while learning the lines for next week's – how did they do that? What a pity that repertory theatre has died, in Derby at least.

Now a final thought on chip shops because I rarely miss an opportunity to stroll down memory lane. When I was a lad, we patronised either Askin's – "Askin For Chips" was their motto – on Burton Road, near the Little City; or an Abbey Street establishment run by a middle-aged couple, the wife a stout woman with plaited blonde hair who reminded me of the female half of *Tristan und Isolde*. Not that I was a particular fan of Richard Wagner operas – more a Guy Mitchell sort of person, really – but our wireless was sometimes tuned to the Third Programme. And that kind of exposure can leave its mark on a small child. Anyway, thanks for the memory, Bernard.

... and from London Road to the Hitchhiker's Guide to the Galaxy

LET'S stay on a theatrical theme for a moment. When he was playing the part of Ford Prefect in the cult television series *Hitchhiker's Guide to the Galaxy*, Derby-born actor David Dixon could explore the weird and wonderful expanse of Douglas Adams's extraordinary, satirical universe. And as a child, he could explore the wonders of his own imagination through the magazines and comics he pored over above his father's newsagent's business on the corner of Hill Street, opposite the old Coliseum cinema.

In 2005, David looked back on those times in 1950s Derby with great affection: "Living in the centre of town meant that the only place to play was above my dad's shop and, along with my brother, I lived in my imagination. We acted out epic journeys across treacherous seas, ice caps, and vast deserts, fighting off pirates, sea monsters, Red Indians and starvation. And there were books to read. Lots and lots of books. And best of all, comics – *Hotspur*, *Victor*, *Beano*, *Dandy*, *Eagle*. We were lucky. We got to read them all for free. Magical."

David was on born on 28 October 1947, at the Nightingale Maternity Home, near his father's shop at 94 London Road. The Dixons later lived at 14 St James's Road, Normanton, a property now used as a Sikh Gurdwara: "My earliest memory of acting is being a shepherd in the Hardwick School nativity play. I had a tea towel on my head, National Health spectacles and a paper palm leaf to wave. One afternoon around that time my dad had, out of the blue, taken me to the Cavendish cinema to see Olivier's *Richard the Third*. Why Dad wasn't at work, why I wasn't at school and why *Richard the Third* I've no idea, but I was the only shepherd with a hump, a withered arm and a limp.

"We left Derby in 1959 for my dad's home town of Nottingham where, later, I studied drama at Clarendon College and then I went on to the Guildhall School of Music and Drama in London"

David landed a small role in the police TV drama series *Z Cars*, quickly followed by his first regular role, in one of the classic drama series of the early 1970s, *A Family At War*. David's youthful appearance, yet mature demeanour, was perfect for the role of Robert Ashton, the 16-year-old naval volunteer trying to assume a man's role while still a boy. In 1981 came *Hitchhiker's Guide to the Galaxy*.

"But remember," said David, "it all started above that newsagent's shop. It was in Derby that the seeds were sown."

Stanley Guy or Guy Stanley?

T HE INTERNET has its critics, but when it comes to tracking down old pals, nothing can beat it. So it was in February 2007 when I decided to find out what had happened to Stanley Guy, an old pal from Becket Juniors. I hadn't seen Stan since we left there in the summer of 1956. It took only a few moments to discover that Stanley Guy was also Guy Stanley. At least that was the name he used when writing bestsellers. After 51 years, we caught up with each other again on St Pancras railway station. I hadn't a clue what Stan would now look like. The last time I saw him he was a snowy-haired 11-year-old. Thus, I approached several startled strangers until Stan spotted me. He took me for lunch at a Japanese restaurant. I later returned the compliment, at the Olde Spa Inn in Abbey Street but, at my insistence, the fish was now cooked and the seaweed replaced by mushy peas.

After he left Derby Technical College in 1963, Stan had gone to work for MI5 (although no one told him at the time), then taught English to Spaniards, and then become a high-flying international banker before embarking on a third career as an author of best-selling crime fiction set in Tokyo, where he now lived for part of the year. I asked him for a contribution to this book. Here it is:

"PEOPLE CALLED celebrities, some barely out of their teens, feel compelled in their ghosted autobiographies to find in their past a history of physical abuse or a fashionable medical condition to draw the readers' sympathy or more likely to somehow offer excuses for their uncouth, gross behavior later in life. It not only insults the real sufferers, it is usually exaggerated, if not entirely invented. Try as I may I can't find a deviant syndrome in my youth, although I sometimes think I deserve one, to help explain my leaving of Derby in 1963, aged 18.

"People are driven from their communities by poverty, famine and war, not forgetting opportunity and adventure. Until the 18th century, in relatively peaceful Britain you were born and died within a few miles, while London teemed with opportunists and refugees from the wars and revolutions on the Continent. Momentum gathered in the 19th and early 20th with the mass exodus of the poor and oppressed for America. When Custer led his 650 cavalry to disaster at the Little Big Horn in 1876, a bedraggled fifth of them were fleeing from war and turmoil in Europe and spoke little English.

"Contemplating my own departure, fleeing war wasn't an issue but I had a good think about abuse, poverty and hunger. If you had not known anything different in those days, it was hard to know if you were poor or not. I like to think we came from a modest background. Clothes, including socks, were repaired, and we certainly didn't go hungry. Abuse was never an issue: we got slapped and whacked but nothing to leave us, as they say too flippantly today, traumatised. Not even my brother, after I watched as a psychopathic maths teacher beat him to the ground with clenched fists.

"When I left Derby for London, in July 1963, the little semi in Rowditch Avenue, off Uttoxeter Road, boasted not a fridge, washing machine, telephone, heating other than two coal fires or an indoor lavatory. No car on the drive, of course. My loving parents were hugely unambitious: mother was a rather embittered, dispossessed farmer's daughter; dad, an army boilermaker content with his cigarettes and little bets on the horses. Life froze for them around 1950 when they left the land for the town. They never went on holiday or took day trips, rarely visited friends or had people round for a meal, never took part in community affairs, bought books or took any interest in our education or future in general. I think they wanted us to be exactly like themselves.

"It didn't bother me that I had to watch the bright lads in the grammar school opposite the house as I trudged to my secondary modern every day, nor when I delivered newspapers to big detached mock Tudor houses on the other side of Uttoxeter Road. I hope I never succumb to recovered memory syndrome, inventing experiences to embellish or excuse my behaviour as many people do when reflecting on their childhood, but for a while I was convinced I was illegitimate, or at least a foundling. I seemed to have nothing in common with my parents and gained no inspiration for the future from them. I spent a lot of time with granddad, the old farmer who lived with us, listening to his glorious tales from the turn of the 20th century and to the wireless we shared while I did my homework. I collected his pension and brought him his pipe tobacco in return for a small supplement to my newspaper and milk round pay.

"Perhaps inspired by his fantastic stories, I became obsessed with plays and the theatre. Half-a-crown got me into the old Derby Playhouse for a new production every two weeks, and in three years I was only turned away once, when Arthur Miller's *View From A Bridge* was deemed too risqué for a lad my age. I sat through a season of Shakespeare's historical plays, mostly starring Robert Hardy, on the flickering Radio Rentals television, following the action with the complete works of the Bard on my lap. I even acted, appearing in the annual school plays and later *College Rhythm* at the old Technical College. One year, an ambitious teacher at Rykneld School decided, for reasons known only to himself, to put on George Bernard Shaw's *St Joan*, a daring project given that ours was an all-boys' school, and I got the lead. Looking at the photos today, me in my blond wig, faux armour and ill-fitting chain mail makes me squirm with embarrassment, even more than reading again the *Derby Evening Telegraph*'s first line in their mostly kind review: "This was failure but not disgrace." My improbable thespian career peaked professionally when I delivered 11 words nightly at the Derby Playhouse in Samuel Beckett's *Waiting for Godot*. I still have the programme, which lists my character as 'a boy'.

"Work in Derby was plentiful in the 1960s, firms competed for our services, even those of secondary modern riff-raff like me, but leaving home and the hometown was not painful. After a working lifetime in Madrid, Tokyo and London, introspection and nostalgia crept slowly into my life, like backache and baldness. An old friend from Tech days, the person who really introduced to the joys of reading, now by far my favourite pastime, contacted me through Friends Reunited and we met after a 30-year gap. Faces change, but it's odd how voices sound as they always did. I also had a look at an internet site listing Derby expatriates and found that a woman I had known very casually in Tokyo and London was actually born in the town. Then, incredibly, author, journalist, editor of this book, primary school pal and Derby lad through and through somehow found me in Tokyo and we met up again in Derby after half a century. I have since strolled the streets of my boyhood with old chums and once again Derby is in my life."

Derby in the Twenties and Thirties

WHEN CHARLES HATTON was a lad, living in Shaftesbury Crescent just after the First World War, he had a profitable sideline every time Derby County played at home. The Hattons had the Rams for neighbours and, like many people living around the Baseball Ground, they took in bicycles at twopence a time. Charles's mother, though, took this homespun business a little further. When I spoke to him in 2004, Charles was 90 and living in Allestree and was one of the few people who could still remember life at the Baseball Ground before it was redeveloped in the late 1920s and early 30s.

He also recalled his mother's entrepreneurial spirit on match days: "Many supporters had cycled from Heanor and Ilkeston, so besides taking in their bikes, my mother made big mugs of steaming tea and ham sandwiches at sixpence a time. Every match day our kitchen would be packed with miners having something to eat and drink before going into the ground.

"One of neighbours tore up his entire garden. It was just trampled-down earth. He could get 100 bikes inside. We all used cloakroom tickets, giving one to the cyclist and sticking the other on his bike saddle for when he came to collect it after the match."

But it is the primitive state of the Baseball Ground that sticks in Charles's memory most: "When my father started taking me to matches in about the 1921-22 season, the "Bob Side, as the Popular Side was then known, was very spartan. You stood on clinker cinders – no doubt Ley's foundry next door was very pleased to get rid of it – and the safety barriers on the terrace were made of wood.

The crossbeam was about three feet long, which was just about enough for me to perch on with my father standing behind, holding me safe.

"The main stand was situated at the Vulcan Street end of the ground – the Normanton end – and contained the players' dressing-rooms and other offices. The players' entrance on to the pitch was directly behind the goal, so they had to run round the back of the net to get on to the field of play. The stand that ran along the Shaftesbury Crescent side of the Baseball Ground was very cramped, no higher really than the houses opposite. Often the ball was kicked over the stand and into the street. Sometimes it would break a window.

Charles Hatton was 90 when I interviewed him in 2004, but his memories of old Derby were as sharp as ever.

"The Osmaston end was simply a clinker bank that had no shelter at all. The houses at the bottom end of Shaftesbury Street and Colombo Street were so near to the ground that people could watch the game from their bedroom windows because there was an uninterrupted view. The groundsman was a Mr Page who lived just round the corner in Reeves Road. His wife washed the players' kit and after a match you could see the shirts and shorts hanging out on the line to dry."

On 4 July 1924, the Baseball Ground became Derby County property when negotiations were completed to purchase it from Sir Francis Ley for £10,000. The clubs' president, Bendle W. Moore, told the club's shareholders at a meeting held at the Royal Hotel a few hours later.

Charles recalled how the club's return to the top flight of English football heralded the redevelopment of the Rams' stadium: "When

Derby were promoted back to the old First Division in 1925-26, that was the start of many great changes at the Baseball Ground. The old stand on Shaftesbury Crescent was demolished and a new main stand – it was later called A, B and C Stands – was erected in its place. It included the dressing-rooms and the offices and was the stand that remained until the ground was demolished earlier this year."

That stand was originally known as "B Pavilion", seated 3,300 people and cost £16,000 to build. "The local Ford and Weston company won the contract to build it," said Charles, "and it totally altered the appearance of the ground, both inside and out."

In 1934, the area was altered even more dramatically when the double-decker Osmaston stand rose up: "About three houses at the bottom of Shaftesbury Crescent and three in Colombo Street were purchased and demolished to make way for the new stand," said Charles. "It also enabled the jitty at the back of the stand to be widened. Originally it was barely six feet wide."

In the 1935 close season, a similar stand rose up behind the Normanton goal, and with extended cover over the Popular Side, the Baseball Ground was unrecognisable from the place where Charles, precariously balanced on a wooden barrier, saw his first football.

"One of the main improvements when the new main stand was built was that supporters had an office they could visit. Previously, season tickets were sold from the window of a house on Shaftesbury Crescent. The club used to rent it for a few days before the start of each season. Two members of staff sat inside, by the open sash window, and the public had to queue up in the street to get served.

"A book of tickets for the 'Bob Side' was 18 shillings [90p] but during the Depression of the 1920s, when thousands of men were out of work, the club used to allow a certain number in free at half-time. When visiting teams arrived at Derby by train, they'd have a meal at the Midland Hotel and then, if it was a fine day, walk to the Baseball Ground with the kit man wheeling his big wicker skip on a sack trolley borrowed from the railway company. Can you imagine Manchester United doing that today? It was a great way to get autographs. I had all the great stars of the day – David Jack, Dixie Dean, Hughie Gallacher, Alex James. I wish I still had them, they'd be worth a fortune I expect."

BACK IN the 1920s, Sundays were sacrosanct. Even people who didn't regularly attend church would observe the Sabbath. Today's Sunday trading, all-day pub opening and wall-to-wall sport would have horrified Derbeians of 80 years ago. Charles Hatton's family was no exception. If his father saw him too preoccupied, he would usually say: "Leave that alone. If you can't find time to do it in six days, you aren't going to do it on the seventh."

So every Sunday, Charles decided to go for a walk instead, and get to know his neighbourhood in greater detail. His approach to whiling away the quietest day of the week left him with a remarkable legacy.

In his 90s, Charles could look back on a Derby where farmers walked their cattle through the town centre. Canal barges unloaded coal just a few hundred yards from the Market Place, the local doctor went on his rounds in an open-topped horse-drawn carriage, and Rolls-Royce tested their cars in the streets around the Nightingale Road factory.

It is a town none of us would recognise today. But to sit down in Charles Hatton's Allestree home, and close your eyes in the company of a man with a seemingly photographic memory, was to take a journey of discovery to see what it was like to live in Derby just after the First World War.

"We lived in Shaftesbury Street, so obviously the Osmaston Road area was very familiar to me. Bradshaw Street – about where Bradshaw Way is today – was a very narrow street, barely wide enough for two cars to pass. Quite often you'd have to stand aside for a farmer herding his cattle down there, on his way to the Cattle Market in the Morledge. In Bloomfield Street there was a police station, run by Superintendent Carter, whose living quarters formed part of the station.

"On Osmaston Road itself there were quite a few large houses occupied by surgeons and senior consultants at the DRI. From Reginald Street to Grange Street there were five large detached houses, each standing in its own grounds. Well back from the road, the middle one was where Mr H. H. Bemrose, of Bemrose's printers, lived. On the opposite side was Derby High School for Girls. On the top corner of Bateman Street was the surgery of Alderman Dr Robert Laurie, who was a mayor of Derby. Dr Laurie was highly respected. In dry weather he used to do his rounds in an open-topped carriage pulled by a horse.

"Next to his surgery was Parr's coalyard, and then another large house, owned by Mr Lemon, who held a very senior position at the Midland Railway Company. At the bottom of Douglas Street there was a nursing home that, some time in the late 1920s, was turned into a Toc H for young men's welfare. In the early 1930s, the section of Osmaston Road between the top of Bloomfield Street and Douglas Street was altered considerably. The road was widened, Dr Laurie's and Mr Lemon's houses, and Parr's coalyard, were all knocked down and the site was then built on by Derby Corporation and became Ivy Square.

"On the corner of Alexandra Street stood yet another very large detached house which was occupied by German POWs in the First World War. In the early 1920s it was replaced by a garage and petrol station. On the opposite side, facing Shaftesbury Street, was a big mill, known as Fletcher's, which employed a lot of young women. Again, in the early 1920s it suddenly shut down and cleared of all its machinery. A few years later it was converted into small business units.

"The railway bridge over the line to Birmingham and Bristol was very narrow with hardly any pavement and just enough room for two trams to pass. About 1928 it was widened to its present size. Off Litchurch Lane, the Midland Railway spread from Osmaston Road to London Road, right up to what is now Ascot Drive. On the opposite side of Osmaston Road was Eastwood Swinglers iron foundry.

"In the early 1920s it closed and lay derelict until the Corporation bought some of the buildings and converted them into a depot for the trolley buses which were introduced into Derby in 1932. On the corner of Abingdon Street stood the tram sheds and this was also the tram terminus, although in about 1924-5, the tramlines were extended to Harvey Road, which was originally just a rough track down to the canal.

"On the corner of Osmaston Road and the road which ran through the Osmaston estate to London Road was the lodge house of the estate. There was a large area of open grassland here, where quite a few churches held their Whitsuntide treats. There were also football pitches, and I remember seeing the world-famous Bertram and Mills Circus here about 1930.

"Osmaston Hall was once owned by the Wilmot family but was later used by the Midland Railway as offices before being demolished in 1938. The church on the estate, St James's the Lesser, was pulled down after the Second World War, I believe. There was a farmhouse on the corner of Osmaston Road and Osmaston Park Road, and the farmland stretched right back to where the Municipal Sports Ground is today.

"The row of houses between the Crown Hotel and Allen Street was just about the centre of Allenton in those days. The middle house had the Derbyshire Constabulary badge over the door. The village bobby lived there and patrolled on his bicycle as far as Shelton Lock. You'd see Rolls-Royce cars being tested around the streets – the drivers wore flying helmets and goggles like First World War pilots – and every year a road race between paper boys from the *Telegraph* and the *Express* passed this way."

In April 1929, after a spell at Hayward's furniture shop on Normanton Road, Charles took a job in the stores of George Fletcher's sugar machinery factory on Litchurch Lane. There he remained, retiring in 1979 after spells as timekeeper – he sounded the "bull" which told workers to report for duty – stock controller and head storekeeper.

Through all this time, his interest in the history of Derby, and his memory, was as sharp as ever: "Some days, we'd go down to the coal wharf at the junction of Derwent Street and Nottingham Road and watch the barges unloading. Imagine that – barges unloading just a couple of hundred yards from Derby town centre. And you know what? It seems like it was only yesterday."

A Derby Christmas, 1930

IMAGINE A Christmas when 12-year-old Scotch whisky cost only 60p a bottle, when plum puddings were less than 7p each, and when you could buy your favourite nephew a toy scooter for around 5p. When there was the immediate prospect of no speed limit for private cars, when Derby County were riding high in the top four of English soccer, and when a diamond engagement ring could be had from a local jeweller's for as little as £2 10s.

Of course, there has to be a catch: this was a picture of Derby over 80 years ago. But whether they were the good old days or not – and Britain was hurtling towards a severe economic depression in the wake of the 1929 Wall Street Crash in the United States, while memories of the First World War were still fresh – December 1930 was a time when Derby folk could forget, for a while at least, their trials and tribulations, and prepare to celebrate another Christmas.

In 1930 the shops of Derby were as brightly lit as ever in the run-up to the festive season. And if those seemingly ridiculous prices were countered by equally low family incomes, most people had managed to put away a few shillings towards a brief respite from the general gloom that clouded Britain. Two local families had an extra boost towards their expenses when they won prizes in the *Derby Daily Telegraph's* weekly beauty contest for mothers and babies. Mrs J Murphy of Broughton House, Shardlow, lifted the first prize of £5, while Mrs E. E. Sherwin of 7 Holmes Street, Derby, took the second prize of £2 10s.

There was less good fortune for a young Derby couple that, on Christmas Eve, visited the public assistance office in Becket Street and asked for a £2 loan. They were astounded to be put through a stringent means test before being refused. As they went away empty-handed, they admitted that they believed they had walked into a Corporation money-lending office.

But what were Derby folk spending their money on, 78 years ago? Shops reported brisk Christmas trade and W H Williamson's, bakers of Franchise Street, were kept busy producing their popular Christmas cakes from 2s each. The Central Educational Ltd in St Peter's Street reminded people that "Christmas cards are fashionable this year"; and Ranby's in Victoria Street offered "1931 goods at 1913 prices".

That Scotch whisky at 12s a bottle could be bought from Severn's in Curzon Street (whose telephone number, incidentally, was "Derby 65"), and George Wood & Son, of Babington Lane, advertised bacon at 1/s per pound, while Derby Co-operative Society had pork pies from 1s 4d per pound. And, if you preferred dining out in the run-up to Christmas 1930, the Cavendish Restaurant in the Cornmarket would serve you up a special lunch of soup, joint and two veg, sweet and coffee for the princely sum of 1s 9d.

Freeman's toyshop on The Spot was selling pedal cars from 13s 11d, scooters at 1s, and dolls from 41/2d to 2s 6d. And any Derby husband who wanted to buy his wife a labour-saving device could find several bargains in the small ads of the *Derby Daily Telegraph*, including a mangle at £1 15s. The columns of advertisements also included a second-hand mahogany-inlaid bedroom suite at £17 and a gramophone at four guineas.

For those with more money to splash out at Christmas 83 years ago, there were opportunities to buy a 1929 Singer Saloon for £125, or a 1928 Riley 9 Monaco Saloon Special (insured until April 1931) for £95.

And for those thinking about moving house, how about a four-bedroomed detached semi in Littleover for a nice round £1,100?

Derby County's Christmas programmes involved two games against Blackburn Rovers. The Rams went down 1-0 at Ewood Park on Christmas Day, but a goal from winger Bertie Mee (who went on to manage Arsenal's famous 1970-71 double-winning team) earned them a 1-1 draw on Boxing Day. That left the Rams fourth in the table, behind Arsenal, Sheffield Wednesday and Aston Villa.

On the sports scene, Derby Ivanhoe topped the Derby Amateur League. Horsley were first in the local Sunday Schools League. And Derby Rovers and Derby Window Cleaners contested the leadership of the Football Favourite League. The *Telegraph Football Special* boasted such by-lines as Major Jinks, who covered soccer, and Stickleback, who was the newspaper's angling correspondence.

Derby's pantomime season opened at the Grand Theatre on Boxing Day, with Randolph Sutton's production of *Cinderella*. The *Evening Telegraph's* drama critic told readers that the highlight was "four real horses which draw Cinderella's carriage". There were nine cinemas from which to choose, including the Hippodrome in Green Lane. The Cosy, on London Road, was showing Ronald Colman in *Bulldog Drummond*, and advertised the "British Thomson Houston Talking Apparatus".

Radio was still in its infancy. On the National Programme on Christmas Day, Reginald Foort played the organ at the Odeon cinema at Marble Arch, and Mr Winston S Churchill made an appeal on behalf of the Wireless for the Blind fund. The radio page in the *Telegraph* announced: "If there is any important news, it will be broadcast at 9pm. Otherwise there will be an interval."

The *Telegraph* reported that George Potter of North Parade had received a second bravery award, this time from the Carnegie Hero Fund, after he stopped a runaway horse outside the tramway terminus on Osmaston Road. The newspaper also told its readers that, by Christmas Day, the Grange estate at Alvaston would be lit by electric light. There was the inevitable sad news. On the Monday before Christmas (which, in 1930, fell on a Thursday), a two-month-old girl was found abandoned on a doorstep in Warwick Avenue. On December 27, Derby Poor Law Authority was still waiting for an offer to adopt the foundling who had spent her first Christmas in Boundary House.

Derby Hospital Report stated that 413 people were "very ill" with diphtheria, and 818 with scarlet fever.

The old and poor of Ashby-de-la-Zouch each received a 10s note pushed through their door by an anonymous donor; and the poor children of Derby benefited from an appeal by the mayor for toys. One donation came from "a lame gentleman who wishes to remain anonymous". Elsewhere, Cardiff City Council banned a concert by the French singer, Maurice Chevalier because they considered his act "too suggestive". In the East End, the Metropolitan Police were hunting a gang of five who had raided a jeweller's shop at gunpoint. The Prince of Wales (later King Edward VIII) abandoned his idea of flying to Sandringham for the Royal Family's traditional Christmas break and instead undertook the journey by car, together with his youngest brother, Prince George. The *Telegraph* called the newly opened airliner route between London and Cape Town "a modern romance". The journey could now be made in only 11 days.

Christmas Day in Derby was wet and warm in 1930, and 0.12 inches of rain fell on the town. Over the Christmas period, cinema attendances were down as folk stayed at home for the holidays. There was no extended holiday, and by December 27 most Derbeians were back at work. They faced a changing world. Acts of Parliament that took effect from New Year's Day 1931 included the abolition of the speed limit for light private motorcars, and the banning of haircutting on Sundays. Under the Hairdressing and Barbers' Shops (Sunday Closing) Act, it became an offence to cut hair or shave a person for profit on the Sabbath. The electors of Rowditch ward took part in their own private poll, organised by Councillor P. C. Cooper-Parry to test their feelings on the town council's proposal to open Derby's parks for Sunday games. The debate became one of recreation ground versus Sunday school, and one protestor told of child gamblers in Derby's parks "playing pontoon and brag for money".

In the wider world there were sinister rumblings. The Nazis had just become Germany's second-largest political party. And in India, Sir Geoffrey De Montmerency, governor of the Punjab, was shot and wounded by two students of Lahore University, who were striving for the sub-continent's independence from British rule. Back in Derby, women flooded to the Market Hall, where Paul's Bargain Spot offered a job lot of "twin-lock combinations" for less than 2s a pair. Clearly, there was a fear that 1931 would be unseasonably cold.

Idyllic
Chester Green Days

IT WAS a late September day in 1923 and Charlie Mozley was pacing up and down the yard of the family home at 33 Old Chester Road. Upstairs, a nurse was attending to Charlie's wife, Edie, who was expecting their second child, a sibling for two-year-old Cliff.

Charlie was trying to take his mind of events by chatting to a neighbour, Mrs Stannard, when the nurse opened the window and announced: "Mr Mozley, you have a daughter." Fifteen minutes later, the window opened again and the nurse called out: "Mr Mozley, you have a son."

At that point Charlie Mozley looked at Mrs Stannard and said: "Blimey, I think I'd better go inside before any more come along."

There were no more, and the Mozley twins, Beryl and Bert, were destined for an idyllic childhood in what was then still a rural part of Derby, where the milk arrived in churns, a schoolfriend lived in a stable, and for twopence, the park keeper would row you across the Derwent. Bert learnt his football on Chester Green and went on to play for the Rams and England before emigrating to Canada in 1955. Today he lives in British Columbia. Beryl, who became Beryl Ford, hadn't moved quite so far, and from her home in California Gardens, she recalled those lazy, hazy days of summers in Chester Green between the wars.

"Our father, Charlie Mozley, was born in Gainsborough but came to Derby as a child when his father was seeking work. Eventually they had a house built on Marcus Street – it's still there, and still called Gainsborough House – before moving to Old

A young Beryl Mozley (far left) playing with her friends in Red Ditch the late 1920s. The brook ran from the River Derwent into Darley Park.

Chester Road. Our mother, Edie Ollernshaw, was born in one of a row of seven cottages called, for some reason, Museum Row, at a right-angle to where they've just pulled down Daniel's works on Mansfield Road."

The Mozleys' childhood was blissfully happy. Said Beryl: "It was like being in the country, one of the nicest places you could wish to live. There were never any problems, no worrying about where the children were. Mother used to pack us sandwiches and we used to play in Red Ditch all day. That's what we called the little brook that ran into the Derwent. For wet days, of course, we had the railway bridge. There was Mrs Tristram's shop on the corner of Kirk Street and Old Chester Road. She made the best fish and chips in Derby, and she also made the best ice-cream in town. In summer I used to walk past, hear the churn going, and could never resist nipping in to ask: 'Can I have a cornet?'"

"On Old Chester Road itself was the farmhouse which was Oliver's farm when my mum was a girl. The farmyard – Manor Yard – is still there. A school friend of mine lived in the stables at the back of the farm, along with her mother, sister and grandfather. I thought it was lovely, so romantic to have a stable to live in. We all used to play in the big barn at the back there. Of course, it's all gone now. Steer's shop was at other end of Old Chester Road. Opposite was a bakery. Prebend House then belonged to Mr Davies JP. His daughter was my Sunday School teacher. I remember going to practise a Nativity play there. I thought it was lovely, like something out of Dickens.

"When my mother worked as a cotton doubler at Darley Mill, she walked through Darley Fields, only in those days it wasn't playing fields, it was pasture land for Bricknall's farm. If there was a Sunday band concert on Darley Park, Mr New, the park keeper, would row us over from Darley Fields for twopence. The Coach and Horses was a little paradise. In the summer, we'd have a walk around Darley Fields on a Sunday evening, and when Dad was flush, he'd say: 'We'll go in the Coach yard.'

"There was an aviary, full of beautiful birds, a pond, a palm tree with a parrot, a monkey. They used to erect a marquee on the

Twins Beryl and Bert Mozley with their elder brother, Cliff. Bert would one day play football for England.

bowling green, from where they sold garden produce from local allotments. The off-sales door was always called the Little Hole. The stables are still there, but I'm afraid the Coach and Horses had lost all its character. Down Alfreton Road, you had Derby Cables, Coleman's and Newtons – and then it was just countryside."

"Mum used to go into town on Saturday evening, when the shops opened late, selling things off. Then it was always Dad's turn to bath us. We had this big bath in front of the fire, and after he dried us, we'd put on lovely cosy nighties, pyjamas and dressing gowns that had been warmed on the fireguard. We went to St Paul's School, next to the chapel. Mr Hallam was the headmaster, but the teacher I remember best was a very pretty lady called Miss Doxey. She met us on the day Bert and I started school – two little four-year-olds clinging to each other – and she was still there when the school closed in the 1960s. She was lovely.

"On the way to school, there were rows of cottages on City Road with little places going off the main road. In the first cottage of one little side road lived an old couple. The wife made sweets and you paid a halfpenny and had a go on a bagatelle board. A high score won you fudge, a low score, bonfire toffee."

In 1932, the Chester Green area bore the brunt of Derby's last serious flood. The Mozleys' house escaped – much to the disappointment of their children: "We wanted to be flooded. Bert, Cliff and I kept running down Alfreton Road to see how far it was coming. We'd run back to Mum and report: 'It's reached Haslam's Lane; it's at Derby Cables; it's up to railway bridge; it's at the top of the street.' Amazingly, it stopped at our front door, and one thing that's always puzzled me is how Dad got his beloved piano on to our kitchen table.

"He was a wonderful pianist, who played at the Coach and Horses and sometimes at the Garden City. During the war, Dad was a captain in the Home Guard and befriended some of the soldiers who were stationed on the anti-aircraft guns on the Racecourse. He'd bring them home from the pub and Mum would make chip sandwiches while the lads played cards and darts We also had many happy hours singing round that piano which Dad had rescued from the flood. One night, two girls knocked on the door and asked: 'Is this Charlie's? Can we come in?' They'd heard the soldiers talking, and thought 'Charlie's' was a social club. I suppose it was, really.

"It sounds odd, but the war was a very happy time because we were all in it together. Mum had five brothers and every time I went out, I met a relative, so I was never scared or alone. A bomb dropped on Bliss's in City Road, and one fell on the railway bridge near Parker Foundry. Dad had always refused to go to the shelter, claiming he'd sleep through any air-raid. But he got up that night.

"These days, lots of parents don't seem to have time to spare for their children. We were never used to our parents going out. Mum was always there when I got home. I feel so lucky to have lived through the times I did, and to have grown up in lovely Chester Green. I can honestly say that I don't have one single bad memory of my childhood there."

Beryl passed away peacefully in her sleep at Littleover Nursing Home on 24 August 2012. She was 88.

Last Tram Clanged Its Way to the Terminus

AS A child Ken Shearwood would watch the final flicker of firelight before falling asleep at his parents' house in Normanton Road. Outside the last tram would clang its way towards the terminus and on Saturday nights the shrill voice of a woman singing in the bar of the Wilmott Arms across the road would penetrate the darkness. It was the 1920s, Derby was an industrial town struggling through a world recession, and as he drifted off to sleep before the dying embers, even a small boy's imagination could not have dreamt up the remarkable life that lay head.

Decorated for bravery in the Second World War, inshore fisherman and successful author, first-class cricketer, a major role in one of the most romantic footballing stories of the 20th century, and 30 years as a teacher at public school, Ken Shearwood has packed more than most into his 92 years.

In 2012, living in retirement at Shoreham-by-Sea, he looked back to those early days in Derby: "My father was a doctor who practised from our family home, an ugly three-storey house which stood next to Christ Church and eventually made way for Derby Labour Exchange

"We had a large garden with a tennis court and a greenhouse full of purple and green grapes. In the summer my parents would give the occasional tennis party, their guests in white flannels enjoying homemade lemonade, thin tomato and cucumber sandwiches and sponge cakes. It was a most incongruous scene amidst the unattractive buildings and noisy road."

Ken Shearwood as a wartime Royal Navy officer, and in more recent times.

In 1940, after prep school at Shardlow Hall and Shrewsbury public school, he went up to Liverpool University to study architecture but a year later enlisted in the Royal Navy. He served on the lower deck in destroyers and then in tank landing craft at the bloody Italy and Sicily landings at Salerno and Anzio. Gaining a command he was awarded the DSC.

Demobbed in 1946 and with no wish to return to architecture, a chance meeting in a Dartmouth pub led to him spending a financially unprofitable but far from unrewarding 18 months as an inshore fisherman off Cornwall. It gave him the ideas for his first two books, *Whistle The Wind* (1959) and *Evening Star* (1972).

Back in 1947, however, and with about as few academic qualifications as it is possible to imagine, he went up to Brasenose College, Oxford, to read history. One of the dons who interviewed him later told him that although he appeared to know no history, he had done a respectable General Paper and that "combined with your close resemblance to a former pupil of ours who we greatly liked and who was killed in the war" had got him in.

Ken captained the university at football, including a game against an FA XI led by Derby County's FA Cup-winning centre-half, Leon Leuty.

He also played first-class cricket for Oxford and in 1949 appeared for Derbyshire against Gloucestershire at Bristol: "It was the days of amateurs and professionals – the so-called gentlemen and players – and along with two other amateurs I found myself staying at a different hotel and using a different dressing-room to the rest of the team. It was most odd. I hit a four off Tom Goddard, which prompted B. O. Allen, their captain who was fielding close to the bat, to belch loudly in my ear, whereupon I was bowled next ball. When we fielded, a swarm of bees descended about the head of Bill Copson, the great Derbyshire fast bowler, who set off for the pavilion, arms flailing and uttering the most fearful expletives as the home crowd called out, 'Windy!'"

It was football, however, that reserved for Ken his greatest sporting moments. At centre-half he was for eight years an integral part of the fabled Pegasus team, the combined Oxford and Cambridge side that won the FA Amateur Cup in 1951 and 1953, each time before crowds of 100,000 at Wembley. One of his teammates was the Derbyshire cricketer and future county captain, Donald Carr. It was one of the game's most romantic stories and gave Ken his third book, *Pegasus*, published in 1975.

By then he was teaching at Lancing College, although when it came to maths he admits he was floundering: "I managed to postpone teaching geometry for three weeks until the answers arrived. Then a know-all in the front row asked: 'Can you do any problem in this book, sir?' "I said that of course I could. So he said: 'Well, can you do the one on page 180?' Summoning up all the nonchalance I could, I copied out the workings and the answer on to the board. It was as meaningless to me as it was to them but everyone seemed satisfied."

None the less, Ken survived at Lancing for the rest of his working life, serving under six headmasters, as master, housemaster, registrar and, eventually, a governor. His fourth book, *Hardly a Scholar*, was published in 1999 and took his story from Normanton Road to retirement in Sussex where he lives with Biddie, his wife of 60 years blissful marriage.

"I was part of the system but while I was proud to have been at Shardlow Hall and Shrewsbury, I was always conscious of the divide between those establishments and the little Christ Church elementary school on the other side of the glass-spiked wall of our garden in Normanton Road. Of course, I've been away from Derby for many years but the memories keep returning. A wet winter's afternoon and a horse and cart coming up Normanton Road, this small stooped figure leading the huge beast along the tramlines, then an organ grinder turning the handle of his hurdy-gurdy outside the dentist's surgery opposite our house. And further down the road a one-legged soldier – a not unfamiliar site in Derby in the 1920s – sits next to his chalk drawings, an upturned cap by his side. My class often asked if I believed in God. I told them that I didn't disbelieve but they had to keep an open mind and remember that small, still voice that speaks at unexpected moments and in unexpected places. I've certainly been very fortunate in my life."

Lew Was a
Good Old Sport

LEW PATRICK no longer got to do any running. Seven years earlier, just after he'd won a half-marathon, his doctor advised him to give up the sport. Lew wasn't happy at the medical advice, but thought he'd better comply. At the age of 83, perhaps his body was trying to tell him something. From his home near Burton Road, Derby, Lew was still indulging in a daily training routine, a familiar figure pounding the streets of the neighbourhood as he tuned-up for yet another event, when he suffered a mild stroke. "I'd just won the veterans' event in a half-marathon when it happened. The doctor told me that it was about time to quit. I'd been running since I was in my early teens and I couldn't imagine giving it up. But if you have any sense, you follow doctor's orders."

Now his 90th year, Lew had to content himself with a thousand memories from a lifetime of long distance running with Derby and County Athletic Club. And if he needed any help in recalling a particular event, he could always consult his large collection of medals and cups, won over a career that spanned almost 70 years. Not that running was Lew's only interest. He also found time play football with a Second Division club, scout for talent for a First Division side, and even play string bass with a dance band.

I'd known Lew all my life. When I was growing up in Gerard Street, he lived just a few hundred yards away, in Harcourt Street. He still lived there and I often called in to sample his homemade wines. On this particular afternoon in the summer of 2003, we settled down with a potent brew made from elderflowers, and then he told me his story.

Lew was born in Warner Street in 1914, the last of nine children. His father was already away serving the First World War. Lew was five before he met him for the first time. Leaving Firs Estate School at the age of 14, Lew went to work at the Carriage and Wagon, alongside Jack Winfield, the English international three-miler, who one day invited young Lew to try out for Derby and County AC at their headquarters at the Wagon and Horses on Ashbourne Road. The young man was soon hooked.

Even into his 70s, Lew Patrick was a familiar figure, pounding Derby's pavements on his training runs.

"Derby and County boasted some of the finest names in British athletics. Besides Jack Winfield, there was Halland Britton, three times AAA ten-mile champions, Paul Abell, the AAA's javelin champion, and Billy Aird, the Scottish AAA's 120 yards hurdles champion. And when the annual Birmingham to Nottingham walking race came through Derby, you could always bet that the first three men would be local lads Harry Ludlow and Harry Taylor, and Tommy Green of Woodford."

In 1940, Lew represented the Midland Counties AAA against Combined Universities in the seven-mile cross-country event, under the captaincy of the great Tipton Harriers and England runner, Jack Holden. "I finished third, but a split-second decision cost me first place. The course included a stream and twice I hurdled it successfully. But the third time round I didn't want to check my stride, so I elected to wade through it. I got stuck and it cost me the race."

Lew also represented the British Railways team against the French Railways in the annual international event, in London in 1948 and 1950, and in Paris in 1949. But he blames his passion for football on the fact that he never won an England vest. "In 1933, I signed as an amateur for Bury, who were then in the Second Division. Their manager, Norman Bullock – who incidentally was probably the smallest centre-half ever to play for England – offered me £3 10s (£3.50) a week to sign professional, but I was earning more than that at the railway works. It would also have cost me my amateur status in the athletics world.

"But I still continued as an amateur, and played in their Central League and West Lancashire League teams. I'm convinced that if I'd concentrated on running, then I'd have won an international vest."

The Patrick family pictured at their Warner Street home in the 1920s. Lew is the little boy on his mother's knee.

He recalled an incident when playing against Derby County Reserves at the Baseball Ground. "I went for the ball with Sid Reid, Derby's Irish international full-back. We hit it at the same time and it burst, which was quite a feat with those old heavy case balls."

Derby County allowed Lew to train with them and it was there that he became lifelong friends with one of the game's greatest players. Jimmy Hagan was then a youngster just starting out in the game. Eventually Hagan fell out with manager George Jobey and moved to Sheffield United, with whom he made over 400 appearances and was capped for England. They kept in touch, however, and when Hagan was married, it was Lew Patrick he turned to as his best man. When Hagan managed First Division West Brom, he signed up Lew as a talent scout. And when he was manager of the great Portuguese club, Benfica, invited his old pal from Derby over to stay with him.

There was an irony in the fact that Lew had turned his back on professional football to preserve his amateur status in athletics. "Even in the pre-war years, 'shamateurism' in athletics was rife. There was one well-known runner from Derby – he's dead now but I won't mention his name because he may still have relatives around – who took £100 from a bookmaker to throw a race. And athletes would sell or pawn their trophies – which were sometimes silver cups, but could also be gold watches or canteens of cutlery. That wasn't allowed, but you have to remember that times were hard. Work was scarce and pay was often poor. People lived on the breadline and you couldn't blame them for looking out for their families."

For many years, Lew also played semi-professionally in a dance band, swam, played bowls and made his own wine. During the Second World War he found time to join the Home Guard, despite working 12-hour shifts in his reserved occupation at the railway.

But running was his greatest passion. "You only get one life and one body – you've got to make the most of both." Coming from a man who didn't run his first marathon until he had passed retirement age, it seems sound advice.

Lew died in 2011, just three years short of his 100th birthday.

Memories of
Bateman Street

BICYCLES, THOUSANDS of bicycles – that was George Quinton's overriding memory of growing up in Derby before the Second World War. George lived at 44 Bateman Street – with a little help from Derby's smallest street, Osbourne Street, a connection between Osmaston Road and London Road – which was the main route for workers going to and from the Carriage and Wagon Works, Rolls-Royce, and Ley's foundry. Hence those bicycles …

"In the 1930s, right through to the early 1960s, few ordinary people owned cars. And so when the workers poured in and out of those factories, there were so many bicycles morning, midday and late afternoon, that a policeman was stationed on point duty at the top of our street. Except during the war, that is, when overtime was essential and those leaving at 8pm and those going on the night shift had to fend for themselves on the road, often in total darkness because of the blackout regulations.

"Bateman Street was my family home for over 40 years, from the early 1930s to the late 1970s. There were 53 houses, a chapel, two builders' merchants, a bowling green, an off-licence, and a coal merchant's yard that had its very own railway siding which also served Jordan's, one of the builders' merchants. The siding was shunted daily; of course, it has now gone.

"But it wasn't just bicycles that made ours a bustling street. It was continuously busy with lorries, buses and horse-drawn carts. The horses drew particularly heavy loads and as they approached the top of the street, they often shed their own loads, which brought the regulars, rushing out with their buckets and shovels to collect garden manure.

"Properties in Bateman Street were mainly two-storey, three-up-and-three-down homes with outside lavatories and no bathrooms. Half a dozen taller, three-storey, buildings at the top of the street are still standing with about six two-storey ones separated only by an entry that led to the backs. All gardens were small and overlooked gardens from properties in Ivy Square, or the railway sidings. On the left-hand side going down Bateman Street, the gardens overlooked those of Barlow Street and have now all been demolished. At the top of the street, one property was demolished as long ago as 1936 and replaced with an area of shrubs. On the other side, the Rolls-Royce Foremens' Club with its own bowling green extended down Bateman Street."

At the bottom of George's Bateman Street was Osbourne Street. It was remarkable that, considering it is Derby's smallest street, in those days it contained a garage for council steamrollers, a gents' lavatory and the Bridge Inn public house.

George again: "Turning into Bateman Street, on the right-hand side was an off-licence run by Jack Brittan and his wife, ably assisted by Mrs Goldington, a member of the family. There was also another family member who ran a very small café in a wall attached to St Andrew's Sidings on London Road. That establishment closed at the end of the war.

"As you came up the street, you passed the homes of Mr and Mrs Lockett and their sons, Mr and Mrs Bird and their two daughters, and Mr and Mrs Pugh and their sons who worked across the road at Jordan's builders yard. The Schofield family, Mr and Mrs Gardener, and the Shardlow family were also on that side of the road. On the other side at the top house was Mr Crabtree, then a family of Smiths, Mr and Mrs Mawday and their son Richard, followed by the Revel family, Quintons, Webb, Brindleys, Anthonys, Browns and Mr and Mrs Quince. Like my father, Mr Quince was an engine driver.

"The Webbs at number 45 was one of the oldest of the street's families. There was Jack Webb and his lovely wife, Rose, and Jack's brother, Arthur, was living with them. There were two other brothers: William Webb, a saddler who had a shop on London Road between Nelson Street and Midland Road, and George Webb, a gardener and property owner who lived in Allenton. Jack's daughter, Olive, left home when she married a well-known Derby headmaster called Mr Timms. She returned many years later to the family home.

"In the early 1940s, Ron Jenkins came to lodge with the Webb family. He, too, was a well-known Derby schoolmaster, at St Anne's in Allenton, at Clarence Road [later Dale] and he later became headmaster of Wilmorton Junior School. Ron had a sad end when he fell down the cellar steps and fractured his skull, never to recover. This robbed him of a retirement he so richly deserved after helping hundreds of boys enjoy so much sport in and out of school hours, but at the same time never neglecting their general education. He was well known as a football referee and played cricket with Derby St Peter's. His proudest moment as a referee was when he took charge of a schoolboy international match at the Baseball Ground when England was captained by Johnny Haynes, who later played for Fulham and the full England team and became the first footballer to be paid £100 a week.

"No review of Bateman Street would be complete without a mention of Jack Brindley and his wife, Hilda. They were very kind people who were always ready to help anybody and were indeed very kind to the Webb family in their old age, and also gave a home to Albert Wild, who was a stranger to them when I introduced him in his hour of need.

"The street was well served by a number of traders, notably Mr Farrant who made his weekly round with hardware items and toiletries. There was also a regular bread deliveryman, and a stop-me-and-buy-one ice-cream man. Those who had a window cleaner were well served by Mr Mowby and his son. There was, of course, the daily milkman. Throughout the war, Mr Redman was our Co-op milkman and he retired when Joe Aldridge returned from service in Burma. Joe had heard of me from Mr Redman and soon invited me to help on his round – remember those happy days before Health and Safety – which I did for many years, continuing on after I started work myself. We were such good friends and remained so until his death midway through his 80s. While he was away on war service he suffered the tragic loss of his own eight-year-old, and in some small way I helped him come to terms with his terrible loss.

"He took me to many Derby County away games and, of course, we went to the Baseball Ground together, as well as the King's Hall for boxing and wrestling and to the County Ground to watch Derbyshire. He was a great bloke, Joe, and people had more that just the Co-op dividend from him. Some needed their coal getting up from the cellar, perhaps a bit of shopping doing for when we called next day, and we also attended to mail they wanted posting.

"Life on the milk round had another side to it for me. I had earlier made friends with the Gibbons family who had the stewardship of the Rolls Royce Foremen's Club. Harold Gibbons was the steward with his dear wife, Dorothy, and they had two sons, Ron and John, and a daughter named Brenda. They were all smokers and when cigarettes were hard to come by, I would get an assortment during our milk rounds and boost my pocket money for my efforts. The Gibbons family was extremely good to me and I thank them for the early opportunity to play billiards, snooker and bowls. The top room of the club premises in Bateman Street was always getting its window broken and it can still be seen today where an iron grid was erected to protect the windows from the swinging trolley poles that regularly came off as the number 33 bus entered the street from Osmaston Road.

"One more abiding memory of helping the milkman is my father arriving home from a night shift and waking me at 6am to say that Joe's float had a wheel off and I was needed as milk and glass was everywhere outside St Andrews Church on London Road. Off I went at high speed, but there was no sign of Joe anywhere. When I reported back home, my father, smiling broadly, said: "Have you checked the calendar?" It was 1 April.

"During the First World War it is recorded that a Zeppelin landed on the bowling green in Bateman Street and to this day the green bears a slight hollow which the home players make good use of. It is interesting that at Number 45 there is a noticeable hump in front of the living room fireplace, which, it is thought, is connected with the Zeppelin. [George is probably referring to the January

1915 raid on Derby by Zeppelins that bombed the Loco Works, Carriage and Wagon Works and gasworks on what is now Pride Park; the damage to which he refers was almost certainly bomb damage, and not a Zeppelin landing].

"The Second World War saw the arrival of smokescreens in the street, the burning of oil and the smell of which will never be forgotten by those who endured it. It was a most unpleasant necessity to assist in trying to safeguard our area and its industries. The screen was no more than a tub of oil with a chimney that often caught fire, which led to the soldiers' mad dash to answer the corporal's shouts of alarm, abuse, anger and much more. But if we kept our doors and windows shut and our keyholes blocked, then all was well in the end. There was an anti-aircraft gun in the Carriage and Wagon Works and it was fired in anger just once, the resulting bits of shrapnel landing on our outside toilet when I was the visitor at about eight o'clock one morning. It did much to elevate constipation. Bateman Street had its own volunteer fire wardens who had regular practices on Sunday morning. I recall one such practice when the powers that be had placed a notice upon one of the taller properties as "being on fire". That wasn't good enough for our regular fire wardens because they had no long ladders. So the notice was moved to a smaller house and 'play' continued as usual. They never did find the culprit who moved the notice and I won't let him down now.

"Some of the properties in the street had their coal cellars reinforced and beds were set up in there for when air raids were in progress. As a temporary measure it was made possible for people to get from cellar to cellar, should the need arise, and strong walls were replaced by a small area of single brick to make it easy to knock through if the exits from the cellar grates were blocked in either properties.

"My own home at number 44 was wonderful and, although I was only a child and a very late one at that, my parents gave me a good start in life and much loving care. I was born too late to know my grandparents but it was explained to me that when I arrived from a Normanton nursing home, my father offered me to Mrs Webb, who became my 'adopted' grandma and a wonderful one at that. My parents already had living with them my mother's brother, Bernard, and a friend, Mrs Mason, who had just come to help my mother with my birth. She remained with us until she died in the 1960s. Bernard left when he got married in 1944. He and his wife, Lena, took me to Wembley for the 1945 War Cup Final between Chelsea and Millwall. What a lucky boy I was and I've been to Wembley many times since, and have many very special memories.

"There were 20 or so children in the street, but they didn't get out to play together with each other because the street was so busy with traffic, even in those days. That didn't stop us visiting friends in their homes, or going to the nearby Arboretum for our recreation. The Arboretum was a haven for children to play and families to enjoy the bandstand, walks around with lovely flowerbeds, fishpond and bowling greens. It was a much-respected place by all and therefore well maintained, even in the war years.

"Playing at home for me meant cards, dominoes, etc. With Uncle Bernard it was cricket and football, according to the season, and both squeezed into a very small back garden. Windows were regularly broken and replaced, and that did cause a problem or two. Notably when I found a hard cricket ball in uncle's bag and took it out for our regular 10-minute lunchtime game and bowled it as a surprise, only for a shocked batsman to send it back on to the ankle of his four-year-old playmate who screamed loudly. Poor Bernard got all the blame.

"Indoors, we had friendly card games with the Webb family and I would visit them to play with Arthur Webb, who was very keen on draughts. My father always played straight, and cheating was a sure way to bring any game to an early end. I remember once when he thought I was trying to see his crib hand and he stopped play and showed me all his cards and declared he would still win, and probably did, for it was early days for me. As a young boy keen to know what his clay pipe was all about, I was spotted looking at it, and a few moments later was told to pick it up and taste it. I can assure any parent that this is a sure-fire way to stop any boy smoking. I have been so grateful for it over the years since that event.

"I was also grateful for his insistence that I found a job of my own choice, provided it had a pension with it. Today, I am so grateful for that too. He had done his best to guide me away from wanting to be an engine driver, by taking me to the door late one night when he was setting off to do night shift and it was snowing hard and very cold. 'Not very nice, son,' was all he had to say.

We lived between two churches – St Andrew's on London Road and St James's on Dairyhouse Road. I'm told that when father decided it was time to marry my mother, in 1931, he wanted a quiet wedding, but because my mother had spent many years helping her mother in a bakery in High Street, it was likely a lot of people would turn up. So father applied for an early-day license and booked an 8am wedding and chose St Andrew's church, known as the railwaymen's church. Word still got around, and over 400 people were thought to be present.

I went to St James's Schools, first in the infants in Madeley Street where Miss Freeman was the headmistress, and then at the junior school in Dairyhouse Road. I missed the era of Mr Tommy Sephton at the senior school, but I did have the pleasure of meeting him in later life and many readers will remember how much he was respected and recall his work at such a good school and later his involvement with the Derbyshire Football Association over many years. His successor, Bob Fletcher, was a good headmaster and I got to know him well when I left school. I joined St James's Church Institute, after being in the church choir for a number of years, and my love for billiards and snooker took off. I also played for the whist teams, which were very successful for many years. The first team was lead by Herbert Brannan, the school caretaker and church verger, and the second team by the vicar, George Mallen. I played for both and it was also customary for a small card school of solo or crib to congregate in the corner of the billiard room whilst waiting their turn for the billiard tables. One evening the vicar was complaining during a crib game that he was not getting any fives in his hands, only the be told he had all four under his foot. All good fun! I give thanks to all my neighbours and my parents for such a wonderful start in life.

Arthur Keily's War

ALTHOUGH MOST Derbeians knew Arthur Keily as a world-class long-distance runner who took part in the 1960 Olympic marathon, when I interviewed him in 2005 I was more interested in another fascinating story that he had to tell. By the time Adolf Hitler invaded France in May 1940, Arthur's war was almost over. Although barely 19 years old, he had already served in three different regiments, had his life saved by his father's actions, and was about to become probably the first British soldier to be evacuated from Dunkirk. That was what I wanted to hear.

Born in Leonard Street, Derby, in March 1921, one of nine children, Arthur came from a military family. His grandfather, James Keily, died of enteric fever whilst serving with the Royal Artillery in India. His father, also Arthur, was born in Rawalpindi and joined the Sherwood Foresters in 1928. So it was not surprising that the young Arthur should also enlist at an early age. Sixty-five years on from his brief but amazing war, Arthur, of Sunnyhill, recalled those remarkable months.

"My father enlisted me in the Foresters' 1st/5th Territorial Battalion on Bonfire Night, 1937, when I was still only 16. One of my brothers, Jerry, and a cousin, Joe, were also in the Foresters, so that was four Keilys doing their bit. I became office boy to RSM C. F. Nicklin, at the headquarters company in the Drill Hall in Becket Street.

"Somehow – don't ask me how – I got into the intelligence section and went on two annual camps, in 1938 to Morecambe and the following year to Holyhead. That summer of 1939 was very tense. Everyone knew war was coming, and, in fact, my father never returned to civilian life. He was called up in late August and promoted to platoon sergeant major, which was then a new rank.

"On 2 September, the day before war was declared, I was also called up. But because I was too young to be posted abroad, I was transferred to the 2nd/5th Foresters, while the 1st/5th, with my father, landed at Cherbourg in November. With the 2nd/5th Foresters, I went from the Drill Hall to the Parochial Hall in Barrett Street, off Harvey Road, near the Blue Peter. Our job was to guard the RAF barrage balloon site at Curzon Lane, off London Road.

"At other times we guarded Rolls-Royce and were billeted in the canteen at the Temperance Hall in Curzon Street. Then we went off to Dove Holes and Chapel-en-le-Frith, to guard massive oil tanks in the quarries there. Eventually we were billeted at Kedleston Hall and it was there, at five in the morning of 31 January, 1940, that I was woken up by a Corporal Litherland and told to get all my kit and report outside.

"I couldn't understand what was going off, but you couldn't argue, so I dressed as quickly as I could and was whisked away in a jeep to the Midland Station in Derby. I found out that I was being compulsorily transferred to the Royal Engineers, to No 1 Railway Training Centre, because, in civilian life, I had been a blacksmith at Derby Locomotive Works. I was eventually posted to the 159 Railway Workshops Company at Longmoor in Hampshire, and in March 1940 was sent on embarkation leave ready to go to France.

"But my mother wrote to my father, and he decided I was too young to be sent abroad, so he pulled some strings. It was a decision that almost certainly saved my life. Had I gone then, I would have been aboard the *Lancastria* when she was sunk off St Nazaire in June 1940, with the loss of over 6,000 men.

"By April 1940, I was back in the blacksmith's department at Longmoor where I suffered a nasty accident when a piece of machinery hit me in the chest. I didn't know it at the time, but I had broken four ribs. I didn't report sick because I'd been posted to 199 Railway Workshop Company, who were about to go to France. This time I was determined to make it and, sure enough, landed with them at Le Havre on 8 May 1940.

"We were moved to the marshalling yards at Rouen, but by then I was in agony and had to report to the MO. I was rushed to a hospital in Dieppe – it had been converted from a casino – and by then I was so run-down that I also had an abscess in my rectum. They operated on me at once. For a few days there were only two other blokes in the ward, but suddenly it filled up with wounded men, on beds and lying on stretchers between the beds. Hitler had invaded France and the Low Countries. The war had started in earnest.

"A medical officer pinned a card saying 'UK' on my chest, and I was taken by ambulance to the coast and put on a hospital ship. It was 18 May. I'd been in France for just 10 days. I often think that I must have been the first soldier evacuated from Dunkirk."

After recuperating in hospital, Arthur was sent to join another railway company, when he heard that his old company, 199, were under canvas at, of all places, Alvaston Park: "Obviously, I asked if I could go there instead, and, after a bit of wrangling, it was sorted out. It was amazing. I walked into the company tent and the RSM said: 'Keily, what are you doing here? We reported you missing.' Then he told me that, the following day, we were all being demobbed to go back to essential war work at the railway. So there I was, 19 years old, evacuated from Dunkirk, and an ex-serviceman in three different regiments. And the war had only just begun."

Alas, there was some tragic news for the Keily family. His father, who had been posted as missing in July, was eventually reported killed in action at Inchville.

"Thanks to the *Derby Evening Telegraph*, in 2000, along with other members of the family, I was able to visit my father's grave, at Inchville communal cemetery. We discovered that he had been killed on the steps of the mayor's office and that the mayor, Henri Berquez, had himself buried him. Monsieur Berquez died in 1956 and is buried only 20 yards from where he laid my father to rest."

There is one last twist to Arthur Keily's war. In June 1959 he received a letter informing him that he had been released from the Army Reserve: "I didn't even know I was still on the reserve. To think, through all those years of building up my running career, I could have been called up at any time. It certainly is a funny old world."

Derby's Tirpitz Raid Aerial Spy

GEORGE WATSON was never quite sure which was his most hazardous moment of the Second World War: searching out the mighty German battleship *Tirpitz*; or being shot at by Derby's Home Guard as he flew over Allestree Park.

It was a mild September day in 1944, when Squadron Leader Watson was sitting on the grass in front of a hanger at RAF Benson in Oxfordshire, enjoying a rare day off from operational flying, and reflecting on his war since leaving the tranquil surroundings of Burnaston aerodrome near Derby. Suddenly his thoughts were interrupted by the sight of a familiar figure approaching. Sixty years later, Mr Watson, then 93 and living in Highfield Gardens, Derby, still had the most vivid memory of the moment that Wing Commander A. H. W. Ball, DSO, DFC, walked up to him.

"It was about midday when the station commander turned up out of the blue and asked if I'd be interested in a special mission. I would have to join up with 617 and 9 Squadrons, who were flying Lancasters. It turned out that they were going to have another go at the *Tirpitz*."

A few days later, George Watson was flying from a remote Soviet naval airfield in northern Russian. His skill and courage that day were vital in an action which saw Hitler lose the last influential ship of his surface battle fleet and effectively marked the end of Germany's naval war.

Mr Watson, a native of Alford, Lincolnshire, had wanted to fly ever since he could remember, and in 1936 he joined the RAF

Volunteer Reserve and was taught to fly at Woodley, near Reading: "In those days we were a territorial outfit and, strictly speaking, were full-time civilian flying instructors. I was working as a flying instructor at Waltham in Lincolnshire, but that operation was closed down and everything moved to Burnaston. I arrived there in September 1939, just after the outbreak of the war, and we were immediately called up. It was three months, though, before we were given uniforms. In the meantime it was blazers and grey flannels."

Newly married and living for a time at the Every Arms, at Egginton, and then on Pastures Hill, George Watson drove to Burnaston every day to teach budding pilots on Tiger Moths and Miles Magisters: "On one occasion, I was hit by the Home Guard while flying over Allestree Park. I was giving them some target practice but I didn't realise they were using live ammunition. On another occasion I had to make a forced landing in a field near a school at Abbots Bromley. Within a minute I was surrounded by about 200 schoolboys."

Mr Watson also caused a security flap at the time of the invasion scare in 1940, when old cars were placed on the runway at dusk, to prevent German aircraft landing: "I was delayed and got back a bit late, just after the cars had been set out. However, I managed to find a convenient path through them and the security people had a quick rethink after that."

After two years at Burnaston, Mr Watson was posted to operation flying with a meteorological squadron based in Norfolk: "We flew high-level Spitfires. Our job was to go out over enemy territory to see if the weather was fit for Bomber Command to do their job. "

From Norfolk, Mr Watson found himself posted to 540 Squadron, which although part of Coastal Command, was based at RAF Benson in Oxfordshire: "We flew Mosquitoes and were a PRU – a photo-reconnaissance unit. We had two main roles. The first was to photograph potential targets for Bomber Command. The second was to revisit the area after the raids to see what damage had been done. It could be pretty hairy work and my motto was: 'Get in, get on, get out.' Sometimes we'd be given high priority jobs – targets that we just had to photograph at almost any cost– and we called those 'dicers'. But I survived. I suppose it was a mixture of good fortune and experience. Don't forget, I was ten years older than most of the other pilots and I'd been flying long before the war."

Throughout the Second World War, Allied air and naval forces had attempted to sink the German capital ship, *Tirpitz*, which, without even weighing anchor, posed a huge threat to the Arctic convoy routes that were a vital supply line between the Western Allies and the Soviet Union. The 44,755-ton battleship, which had a crew of 2,400 men, had been commissioned at Wihelmshaven in February 1941 and as flagship of Germany's Baltic Fleet, had first operated in the Baltic, including combat missions connected with Hitler's invasion of the Soviet Union.

George Watson, pictured with some of his wartime memorabilia.

Her sister ship, the *Bismarck*, was found and sunk by the Royal Navy in the North Atlantic, but the *Tirpitz* proved elusive.

In January 1942, the *Tirpitz* sailed to Norwegian waters, where she was to spend the rest of the war. The mighty battleship anchored first at Trondheim, and, on 30-31 January, seven British Stirlings of 15 Squadron attempted to attack her in Faettenfjord but failed to locate her. In March, returning to Trondheim from an aborted operation to intercept British convoys, the *Tirpitz* came under air attack for the first time when 12 Albacore torpedo biplanes of 817 and 832 Squadrons from the carrier HMS *Victorious* swooped down on her. The battleship avoided all the torpedoes and shot down two Albacores. In the afternoon the *Tirpitz* was safely anchored in Vestfjord, near Narvik.

A few days later she returned to Trondheim and within two weeks was under attack again, this time from 33 Halifax bombers. Again the raid was unsuccessful and six aircraft failed to return.

There were two attempts in April. Yet again the *Tirpitz* was not hit and the RAF lost a further seven aircraft. The sinking of the *Tirpitz* was becoming something of an obsession for the Allies, although she never actually came into contact with any Allied shipping and fired her guns at enemy targets only once, during an Allied raid on shore facilities at Spitsbergen in September 1943.

That month three British submarines in Kaafjord attacked her. Two mines, each of two tons, were placed under the battleship's keel, and at last the *Tirpitz* was seriously damaged. She was out of action for the next six months. One German sailor lost his life and 40 were wounded. The three midget submarines were all sunk.

Fully repaired, however, she became a priority target once more. In February 1944 she was attacked, without success, by four Soviet bombers. Finally, in April, 40 carrier-based British bombers hit her 14 times, killing 132 of her crew and wounding 316. In August, Barracudas from Royal Navy carriers managed three separate raids on the *Tirpitz*. They hit her twice, but there was no serious damage.

The RAF now turned to a new weapon, the Tallboy bomb designed by Ripley-born Barnes Wallis, who had invented the "bouncing bomb" for the Dambusters. Each Tallboy weighed 12,000lb, had 5,200lb of high explosive, and was designed for accurate flight and great penetration.

The first major hurdle was that Kaafjord in Northern Norway, where the *Tirpitz* lay, was well out of return range of Lancasters flying from Britain and carrying Tallboy bombs. It was decided that both 617, "The Dambusters", and 9 Squadron would fly to a base in Yagodnik, an island airfield in Northern Russia, refuel, and carry out the attack from there.

Enter George Watson, lately of Burnaston aerodrome in Derbyshire: "The weather was poor and it would be my job to fly over the fjord every day until conditions improved sufficiently for the raid to go ahead."

Refuelling at Lossiemouth and then flying over Norway, Sweden and Finland, Mr Watson then had the difficult task of locating the Russian airfield in a flat, featureless landscape. Several Lancasters had already missed the landing strip and were inextricably stuck in marshy ground.

Nearing his destination, Mr Watson had to locate the log cabin "city" of Archangel, by which time the cloud base was so low that he was flying at rooftop level.

"I was at about 27,000 feet and saw a huge weather front ahead, so I decided to keep it visual. It's a good job there weren't any tall buildings in Archangel because I was down to 300 feet. We'd been told to find a lake to the north-west of Archangel and fly around that, otherwise we would be shot at. We'd also been told to make radio contact, but there was a problem with the Russian radio transmitter.

"I had a problem in that my navigator, Mac, was a lovely man but wasn't very good at map-reading. I never did find the lake but I followed the River Dvina and eventually we were on the ground at Yagodnik. It was a Godforsaken place, just a few wooden bungalow-type buildings. Someone, though, had thoughtfully hung out a banner proclaiming: 'Welcome to the Glorious British Fliers'".

By this time Mr Watson had another problem. An abscess on his left hand had become poisoned, which meant that he would have to make 1,300-mile round trip to find the *Tirpitz* virtually one-handed: "I hadn't got any choice. I was the only Mosquito pilot for thousands of miles."

Mr Watson went out every day looking for a break in the weather over the *Tirpitz*. "I couldn't get too near because the Germans would have been alerted, but on about the fourth day the weather cleared a little and I thought the bombers could go in. The timing was so critical that I hadn't got time to land and report in – and there was still no radio contact. So I dived low over the airfield to signal 'go', and the Lancasters were taking off before I landed."

On 15 September, 1944, 27 Lancasters, carrying 20 Tallboys, set off at George Watson's signal. With mountains screening the Lancasters' approach, the Germans were taken by surprise and the *Tirpitz* was late in getting her smokescreens up. One Tallboy smashed straight through the *Tirpitz's* forecastle and burst deep in her hull. The shock waves from this bomb, and from near misses, also damaged the ship's engines. All 27 Lancasters returned safely to Yagodnik, but George Watson was already back over the target.

"I had just got back from flying 650 miles there and 650 miles back, most of it one-handed, and the CO said: 'Do you think you could go again?' I asked my navigator: 'What do you think Mac? Can we go again?' He just shrugged and grunted: 'I suppose so.'

"This time we had to assess the damage and, of course, apart from having to go in much closer, the Germans were expecting us. When we got over the *Tirpitz*, the weather had closed in again and it was impossible to take any useful pictures. So I decided to find a hole in the cloud, go down and have a look. I spiralled the aircraft down and Mac tried to make an assessment. I'd never seen so much flak before, and I never saw as much again. I read later that there were 45 heavy gun emplacements around the *Tirpitz*. It felt as if every one of them was shooting at me."

The Germans decided to move the *Tirpitz* to a shallow birth near Tromso, where she could not be sunk, but the RAF, unsure of how successful the Tallboy raid had been, mounted two more raids. In October little further damage was done to the battleship, but on November 12, 1944, the *Tirpitz* was hit again and, as the result of an internal explosion, the mighty battleship rolled over to port and capsized.

However, a German document found after the war confirmed that the raid in which George Watson had played such a key role, had already done the job: "It was estimated that repairs, even if they could be carried out without interruption, would take at least nine months ... it was eventually decided on 23 September, 1944 that it was no longer possible to make the *Tirpitz* ready for sea and action again..."

For his part in Operation Paravane – the codename of the September raid on the *Tirpitz* – George Watson was awarded the DFC.

In December 1945, he was demobbed and came to live in Derby.

"Derby Flying Club offered me a job as a flying instructor, but the money wasn't very good so I worked for a London-based manufacturing company for a while and then, in later years until I retired, as a manager for Kennings in Derby. I obviously kept an interest in flying after the war, but mostly for recreational purposes. Why did I get involved in flying all those years ago? I don't really know. Because I was a bit stupid I suppose."

The Day Peace Broke Out

THE *EVENING Telegraph* newspaper seller hurrying through Derby Bus Station was doing a passable imitation of the Pied Piper of Hamelin. Hundreds of people flocked after him and within two minutes of receiving his latest supply of papers, he had sold out. Sixty-eight years later, many of those newspapers survived, souvenirs of one of the most momentous days in British history – Tuesday, 8 May, 1945, VE Day – their headline signalling the end of the war in Europe.

After six long war-weary years, 148 air-raid alerts, 152 high-explosive bombs, 164 incendiary bombs, 45 civilian deaths due to enemy action, and between 3,000 and 4,000 of the town's houses damaged, for the people of Derby the end was near. The memories, though, are still fresh, particularly memories of that fateful Sunday of 3 September, 1939, when war was declared. Even today, Jim Phelps, now retired and living in Derby's Highfield Estate after many years as the city's assistant recreation officer, remembers that weekend as if it was yesterday:

"I was only nine and it was all so exciting. On the Saturday night, I stood in the doorway of my mother's fish and chip shop in Sacheverel Street and watched a spectacular thunderstorm bring five balloons crashing down in flames. One fell on a power cable and plunged a large part of the town into darkness for about three hours.

"I went to bed on the Saturday, wondering what the morning would bring. At 11.15am we tuned in our wireless and heard the Prime Minister, Neville Chamberlain, announce that we were at war. I ran into the street to find my pals. Then I saw some of the neighbours. They could remember the last war. They were weeping. Suddenly, I realised what it meant."

Jim spent the remainder of the day helping to fill sandbags on Burton Road as Derby prepared for the worst. And there was worse to come.

Later in the war, Fred Gifford, who then lived in Ellesmere Avenue, Wilmorton, was a station officer in Derby's Auxiliary Fire Service and nightly found himself defying bombs and falling buildings as he helped to fight fires at the height of the blitz. Even on the nights when Derby itself escaped the bombing, there was no respite for Fred and his colleagues. As the Luftwaffe rained death upon British cities, the AFS would be rushed to tackle frightening blazes elsewhere. On one occasion, AFS men from Derby fought oil fires at Thameshaven for three days without respite.

Fred Gifford recalled: "Often we'd arrive in a town as complete strangers and be directed to our own particular fire through streets ablaze on either side. Then we had to find the nearest water supply and get on with the job. Twelve-hour shifts were a nightly

Troops outside Derby Midland railway station,
being inspected by the Duke of Devonshire in 1941.

occurrence and map reading was essential, as all the road signs had been removed in case of an invasion. It was very hairy. Often we'd fight fires with bombs falling all around us.

"There were lighter moments, of course. Before the war I was the signalling examiner for the Boy Scouts and, using the boys who had passed the test, I evolved a scheme for a chain of communication of visual signalling from Jury Street to the outer fire stations

"Using the Cathedral tower, we were able to make contact with all the stations with Morse code and flags. It caused a sensation and one day the trapdoor opened and a policeman stuck his head through and asked: 'What's going on here?' With the co-operation of the Sherwood Foresters stationed on Markeaton Park, and using their daylight signalling equipment, we enlarged the scheme. But we could only loan the Foresters' equipment, so Station Officer Raynor and I experimented with car sidelights and batteries. It was never used, but the number of times we were reported for 'signalling to the enemy' was amazing."

There were, indeed, lighter moments. For Alex McWilliams, who was working at Rolls-Royce, the war years brought out the best in people:

"Without doubt there was something indefinable about life in Derby at the time. We weathered the very worst that the Germans could throw at us, and things were beginning to level out a bit. We couldn't actually see any light at the end of a very long tunnel, but at least we had begun to feel our way around in the gloom.

"I suppose it was because we all had something to fight for, and we had a common enemy. Men and women got up and went to work for long shifts, went home to snatch some sleep, and then back to work, or perhaps on to Home Guard duty. They didn't grumble. There was a job to be done and they just got on with it. It was an attitude that spilled over into everything we did, even sport. When we played football or cricket, we played it hard but we played it fair. People knew that, ultimately, we were all on the same side."

In early May 1945, people knew it could be only a matter of time before peace was announced, and they gathered around their wireless sets all over Derby. The first news that the end had come was heard, ironically, through German radio.

Everyone knew that the German surrender was imminent and by mid-morning there were already 2,000 people in Derby Market Place before a violent midday thunderstorm sent them scurrying for cover.

The Bishop of Derby reminded them: "We have won a victory over Germany. Be satisfied with that. Don't grumble about the weather."

By 2pm, the sun was shining again and the victory celebrations went into full swing. Trolley bus standards were swathed in bunting, and loudspeakers replayed speeches by the King and Winston Churchill, the Prime Minister.

Amateur musicians armed, with saxophones and accordions, were joined by others with dustbin lids, tin cans and anything else that would make a noise. One US military policeman was surrounded and had all his equipment removed while a saloon car was pushed around the square before being ripped to pieces. The crowd's repertoire seemed to consist of just three songs: *There'll Always Be An England*; *Pack Up Your Troubles*; and *Roll Out The Barrel*.

At the Plaza ballroom, police were called to eject hundreds of gatecrashers to Sam Ramsden's private party at which George Elrick, later to win fame on television's *New Faces* talent-spotting programme in the 1970s, was playing with his band.

Street parties lasted all week. In Stockbrook Street blackout material was burned to the solemn accompaniment of a gramophone wheezing out *There'll Always Be An England*, and in Agard Street, on the edge of Derby's West End, a piano was wheeled into the street.

On Osmaston Road, a shopkeeper had effigies of Hitler and Goering hanging from his premises, while in Brook Street another Hitler dummy bore the sentiment: "Adolf, you've had it."

By midnight on 8 May, 1945, it was impossible to estimate the number of people who had thronged the Market Place. In Green Lane, the Beaconsfield Club had to enlist the help of the NFS turntable ladder to raise the Union Flag on the building's flagpole. The other option, climbing out on to the roof via an attic window, was declared to dangerous.

The violent midday storm broke up a British Legion parade following a service at St Werburgh's Church. It erupted as the parade passed the Mayor and Mayoress of Derby, Councillor and Mrs W H Phillips, and Lt-Col C. C. Stepney, who were taking the salute in the Market Place.

The wind whipped off hats and the downpour soaked hundreds of people. The participants held fast until they had passed the saluting base, and then dived for cover. The British Legion Band stopped half way through the march and dashed into a shop doorway until the worst of the storm had abated.

The residents of Norman Street in New Normanton collected £90 for their party and everywhere carefully stored-up rations were at last unwrapped as the parties began. Both the Midland Station and the Cavendish were also decorated with bunting and flags.

The first weather forecast since the outbreak of war was published on 4 May. It had predicted "sporadic outbreaks of rain and the possibility of thunder". The peak temperature was reached on 9 May when the mercury rose to nearly 72 degree Fahrenheit.

By then Darley Park looked more like Blackpool beach at the start of the season; there was a three-and-a-half-hour wait for rowing boats on Alvaston Lake; at the Arboretum, 7,000 happy people watched the Searchlights Concert Party; and 3,000 flocked to Normanton Park to hear the Derby Borough Military Band.

There was football, too. Peter Doherty scored both goals for Derby County when they drew 2-2 with neighbours Nottingham Forest in a victory match. A crowd of almost 7,000 saw the game at the bomb-damaged Baseball Ground, among them the coal merchant from Horsley Woodhouse who, later that month, was find £1 10s £1.50) by Derby magistrates for "misuse of petrol". His crime? He had driven his son to the Baseball Ground to watch the Rams. The magistrates were not attempting sarcasm; it was simply that in the days when posters asked: 'Is Your Journey Really Necessary?' watching football as hardly considered essential.

For those who wanted to get indoors on that hot, humid week, there was a choice of 16 cinemas in Derby, showing films ranging from Joan Fontaine in *Frenchman's Creek*, adapted from the Daphne du Maurier novel, at the Hippodrome (the theatre in Green Lane then enjoying a new career as a cinema) to James Cagney and Humphrey Bogart in *The Roaring Twenties* at the Cosmo in Upper Boundary Road.

There was also one theatre, the Grand in Babington Lane, where the Ballets Jooss Company held their own quiet celebration backstage after their production had finished for the evening. Before the show the national anthems of Britain, France, the United States and the Soviet Union were played.

Yet in the midst of all this euphoria there was some bitterness towards the Government after the people had heard news of Germany's unconditional surrender from German sources only. As each hour past, there was still no official announcement from the British Government as the mood of excitement changed to one of impatience.

As the *Evening Telegraph* put it: "Let's have news that it's VE Day and be done with it!"

In Derby Market Place, a Trent bus conductress, on hearing that the Germans had announced their surrender, proclaimed: "That's good enough for me. I've got a day off!" But a man nearby grumbled: "We've got it from every country in the world – except our own." Some LMS workers decided not wait and downed tools. Company officials held a hasty meeting and decided to let the workers go, except for those doing essential work.

It had been known for some days that the end was imminent and on 4 May the *Derby Evening Telegraph* had announced that on "VE Day Plus One" it would not publish. Uncertain whether the holiday announcement applied to them, many workers turned up, only to be sent back home. Outside the Rolls-Royce factory in Nightingale Road, workers strolled in groups, discussing how to spend the rest of the day.

The confusion had arisen by a change in arrangements when, because VE Day itself had been announced so late, so the following day was also declared a holiday. Departmental heads at Rolls-Royce eventually decided that work should begin again with the night shift on the Thursday. At teatime on VE Day, the Harrison family of Middleton Street received a great surprise. Through the door, to the delight of his wife and family, came Corporal "Sid" Harrison of the RASC. Forty-four-year-old Corporal Harrison had made his way home from a German PoW camp, where he had been since his capture in 1941.

Throughout the week the people of Derby had been seeing the first evidence of one of the most terrible episodes in European history as newsreels in cinemas across the town showed scenes recorded by army cameramen entering the concentration camps at Belsen and Buchenwald.

For the people of Derby, the Second World War had ended, in Europe at least, but it would be some time yet before the revellers could put their minds to turning victory over Hitler into a lasting peace. Many of them had husbands and sweethearts, sons and brothers, still fighting the Japanese in the jungles of the Far East. It was not until the explosion of two nuclear bombs over the cities of Hiroshima and Nagasaki, three months later, that Japan surrendered. And even then it would be some months before the troops began to return home.

There were many happy homecomings, of course, but for many more the world would never be the same. Years of fighting or captivity, often in the most barbaric conditions, had changed them; and in different ways the war had also changed the ones they had left behind.

VJ Day – Victory over Japan – on August 8, 1945, was about as confusing as VE Day. Most people assumed that the second victory holiday of the summer would not begin until the Thursday. So the majority did not hear the Prime Minister's midnight announcement and awoke uncertain as to whether this would be just another normal day.

The result was that hundreds set off for work as usual. Not until the victory peals were sounded by the Derby Cathedral bells did they realise the war really was finally over. Housewives rushed to town to queue for fish, meat, bread, and even flags. By 9.30am demand for bread was so great that bakers were restricting supplies to one loaf per customer.

There were angry scenes outside the Co-op's main store in East Street. It was closed and many of the women had not drawn their weekly rations of fat and other cooking requirements. A queue of

*August 1945 and crowds in Derby Market Place celebrate the
end of the war in the Far East.*

60 women waited for the Co-op offices in Albion to open so that
they could draw their "divvy", only to be told that the Co-op would
be closed for two days. Of 180 Corporation bus employees on the
early shift, all but 50 turned up for work. Buses ran to take night
shift workers home, and staff to the City and Isolation Hospitals,
before the bus crews themselves were stood down for the rest of
the day.

With two-day leave passes in their pockets, hundreds of
servicemen and women head for the LMS Station, where queues for
trains stretched down Midland Road as army and RAF personnel
from bases around the town tried desperately to get home in time
for the victory celebrations.

There had been scenes of wild excitement in the early hours of
the morning outside Normanton Barracks. The midnight broadcast
had been the signal for merrymaking and ATS girls stationed there
had donned overcoats over their nightclothes and spilled out of the
depot to celebrate. Members of the Sherwood Foresters band drew
their instruments and soon a dance was in full swing on the barrack

square as hundreds of nearby residents came out of their houses to join in. The vicar of St Giles's Church on Village Street arrived and civilians and soldiers joined in a service at the gates to the barracks.

Men on night shift at the Carriage and Wagon Works heard of the surrender and decided to leave work for "a couple of hours of jollification". When official sanction was denied them, they simply dragged the canteen piano into one of the sheds and began a singsong that lasted until dawn. And a truckload of black American troops made merry by "careering around the town centre shouting and singing".

The arrival of non-white troops in the Derby area had caused some needless friction. In August 1997, Elsie Church told her grandson, Peter King: "In Derby when the Americans came, the black Americans came and the white Americans came. In Derby they had separate nights for them both to be out. They never let both the black and the white Americans in town together, because there was still a bit of tension. They were lovely boys the black boys were. You had nothing to be afraid of. They were good lads."

On VJ Day, there were plenty of street parties. In Rivett Street, 30 children enjoyed home-made cakes and buns; the major feature of the party in Melbourne Street was a 7lb iced "Victory Peace Cake" made by Mrs Ethel Wright; old age pensioners were invited to a children's party in King Alfred Street and enjoyed fruit, jelly, cakes and buns.

In Goodwin Street, 161 happy faces testified to the quality of the fare bought by the £9 5s collected for the occasion; children in Offerton Avenue burned an effigy of the Japanese warlord Togo; the anti-aircraft battery on Kingsway loaned their canteen so that the children of the Westleigh Estate could stage their party.

And on Chester Green there was a football match between local men and women who swapped clothes for the occasion. At St James's Road School, the problem of finding enough fat to bake cakes was solved when Mrs H. Rawlings went round the neighbourhood to beg a piece of margarine "the size of a walnut" from each resident. Soon she had enough to begin work. At midnight in the Market Place, a huge crowd sang *Abide With Me* before falling into a two-minutes silence to remember the dead.

Earlier, thousands had danced to the accompaniment of the Rolls-Royce Band, which competed with several impromptu "orchestras" around the square.

In December 1945, Jim Phelps was now 16. On Christmas morning he went to Rosehill Methodist Church on Normanton Road where there were some German prisoners-of-war in the congregation.

They sat shoulder to shoulder with their fellow worshippers, some of the ordinary people of Derby, and together they sang *Silent Night*.

Jim said: "My mind went back to that September day when war was declared and I thought about all the horror, the hurt and heartache. And then I wondered what we had learned, and what tomorrow would bring."

A Sherwood Forester and a Missing Crest

IN THE spring of 1947, George Wright has just settled back into his job at the CWS paint works in Stockbrook Street, Derby, when he received a visit from a second lieutenant in the Sherwood Foresters, the regiment from which George had been demobbed a few months earlier. Colonel Stuart Carter wanted to see him at Normanton Barracks. What could the CO want? After five years with the 2nd Battalion, in action from Tunisia, the Anzio landings, fighting right up the boot of Italy, and then Palestine and Iraq, George thought he had left the army behind. He certainly couldn't think of any unfinished business. Ushered in to see the colonel, he discovered the nature of his special mission.

"We had a chinwag," said George, who, when we met in July 2005, was living in Sunart Close, Sinfin Moor, "and then the colonel told me that we wanted me to produce a large copy of the regimental crest, complete with battle honours. He'd asked me because part of my army duties had been signwriting. I asked him where I should send the bill. He laughed and said he thought I'd do it for the glory of the regiment. I said that after five years fighting with the Foresters, I thought I'd done my bit. But I set to work all the same. All I had to go on was a small badge, but it finished up about four feet by three. I did the whole lot, even made the frame. The colonel said it was intended for the old comrades' association headquarters at Bakewell, so I handed it over – and that's the very last time I saw it, nearly 60 years ago.

"Earlier this year, I happened to be showing a photograph of it to some ex-Sherwood Foresters, and a couple said they had seen it in Bakewell Church. So about a month ago, I went to look at it. But it had gone. The place where the old comrades met is used for something else now, so that's perhaps when it was moved to the church. But the curate searched high and low, and couldn't find it there. Now we're trying to locate it. The feeling among the old comrades is that it ought to be on display at Derby Cathedral, where the 1st Battalion has its crest, but our 2nd Battalion isn't represented. After all we went through in the war, it would mean a lot, especially for the memory of the lads who never came back."

George was born in Alvaston in December 1922 and went to Brighton Road School before starting at the paint works when he was 14: "I only had two days' Christmas holiday in 1936, he recalled. "I left school and started work almost immediately. I stood only 4ft 6ins in those days, a little lad sent into a man's world."

Five years later, George was catapulted into an even bigger world when he was called up during the Second World War: "It was January 1942. I enlisted at Normanton Barracks and got involved in a new venture. Instead of being sent to a holding battalion, all the new lads were sent straight to a recruits' company at Caister camp, near Great Yarmouth. After six months there, and six months in Scotland doing assault landing craft training, we were sent to North Africa. We came straight off the troopship in Tunisia and immediately did a three-mile forced march through mud and slime.

"My dad had been at Ypres in the First World War and, before I left, he'd said: 'Your war won't be like ours, lad. Ours was all mud and dirt.' But he didn't know about the gullies and wadis in North Africa, all grey mud. It was awful. We were part of the British North Africa Expeditionary Force. Our role was defensive. Wherever trouble broke out, we'd be sent to deal with it. Eventually, the North African campaign was over and we were sent to Italy. First of all we did a landing at Pantelleria, an island between Tunisia and Sicily.

"I was as sick as a dog on the landing craft, it was so rough. To be honest they could have come and captured the lot of us there and then. But the only man who was injured broke his ankle jumping ashore. Then we looked up and saw the American bombers overhead, so many of them that their wing-tips were almost touching. That night we went on a recce and discovered the extent of the bombing. Every bomb hole was overlapping other bomb holes. When it came to Anzio on the Italian mainland, early in 1944, that was a bloodbath. We went in with the Americans on one side. I was forward infantry but I was in a tank landing craft, with infantry landing craft either side.

"One them shuddered to a stop and the men inside thought they were on the beach, so they dropped the ramp – and stepped into 12 feet of water. The craft had hit a sand bar. They were all in full kit. I don't know how many drowned. Then the Germans started shelling their landing craft, blew it to smithereens. We were carrying 23 Churchill tanks and I thought, blimey, if we get hit, we've no chance. Our driver never bothered to turn round. He just reversed, flat out, a full three miles out sea, backwards.

"But Anzio was bloody. We finished up with about 100 men out of perhaps 1,300. The rest were killed, wounded or captured. Those of us who were left were reformed with the Black Watch. Although I was infantry, I was also in a specialist company that went ahead to

George Wright pictured in his days as a Sherwood Forester.

prepare for the rest of the battalion whenever we moved. We did everything, from digging latrines to searching for and detonating explosives. When we took over a house as an HQ, we had to go in first and search for booby traps, make it safe for the officers

"Eventually we got up to Rome, Florence, and then Turin. It was Christmas by then and we were looking down the valley when a German shouted up to us: 'Happy Christmas, Tommy.' So we shouted back: 'Happy Christmas, Fritz.' By then, no one could move because of thick snow. It was quite a shock after North Africa. Then, four days later, we were in Palestine. Later on, we also got into Iraq. It was much the same as today – being ambushed on patrol.

We went to Syria and came home from there. I was demobbed at Beverley in December 1946.

"We saw many terrible things – men blown in half, things like that – but we got no counselling. Just a demob suit and a travel pass, and we were left to get on with the rest of lives. And after 99 days' leave – I only took 94 actually – I went back to the paint works. For £4 16s 6d for a 48-hour week, by the way."

"Anyway, that's when I got the call to paint the regimental badge. After all we went through, I would love to find that and see it on display, in memory of all we did." After the CWS paintworks, George moved to the Qualcast car division in 1960, where he remained until he retired in 1987. I don't know if he ever tracked down his missing artwork.

Freddie Naylor, the "Fighting Midget"

WHEN SEVEN-YEAR-OLD Freddie Naylor boxed an exhibition match with his elder brother at Derby Drill Hall in Becket Street in 1921, he could never have imagined that, one day, he would appear on the same bill as a world heavyweight champion. Young Freddie and his brother, Samuel, went on to fight exhibition bouts all over England, and were billed as the "Fighting Midgets", before Freddie turned professional and began a career in which saw he had 350 fights, many of which came after he had joined Derby Borough Police.

But, long after he had retired from boxing, and from the police, it was a night at the Victoria Baths, Nottingham, which stuck most in his mind. Also boxing that night in 1937 was the remarkable "Ambling Alp", the giant Italian, Primo Carnera, who, three years earlier, had shocked boxing by knocking-out world champion Jack Sharkey.

Before his death in 1998, Freddie Naylor told me about that night: "Top of the bill was Don McCorkindale, the South African heavyweight champion, who was fighting Harry Crossley of Britain. I was fighting an American called Kid Burke, and the strange thing was that every fight on the card that night ended in the third round. I knocked Burke out, incidentally."

"Then Carnera fought three one-minutes rounds each with three British champions, including Tom Berry, the cruiserweight title holder. Afterwards, Carnera gave a demonstration of his physical fitness. He was a former circus strongman who, to be honest, had been manufactured by unscrupulous promoters with a lot of weak opponents to get a title shot. But he had knocked out Sharkey and, although there were mutterings that Sharkey had taken a dive, the fact was, he was world champion. He was also a fantastic athlete. And despite being six and half feet tall, and weighing well over 18 stones, he was a light on his feet as a featherweight."

Boxing was in Freddie Naylor's family. His uncle, Harry Curzon, was heavyweight champion of India when he was in the Army. After his demob, Derby County signed Curzon to put the Rams

Freddie Naylor in his fighting prime

players through their paces. After his early years as boxing "midget", Naylor turned to the Saturday night boxing booth that stood opposite Derby Bus Station: "I was only 14 and used to earn five shillings for lasting six rounds. When I was 16, I got my professional licence and earned about £5 a fight, which was big money in those days. The birth of professional boxing in Derby was at the Highfield club on Ashbourne Road, run by Frank Woodhouse who went on to manage me."

Naylor was the first boxer of any prominence that Derby had produced. But at the age of 21 he smashed a knucklebone and that put him out of action for four years. He joined the Derby police and, at the age of 25, eventually made a comeback in the ring, when he fought Chuck Parker, a British welterweight contender, and lost on points. Defeat it may have been, but his performance that night convinced him that he still had a future in the ring. Naylor helped coach the Derby police boxing team, which vied with Nottingham as one of the best in the country.

"We had my old friend, Horace Smith, who became police middleweight champion of Europe. And the Notts team had Arthur Beaves, the European heavyweight champion. Between us, we had some of the best amateur boxers in the business."

Naylor lost only one of his first 100 bouts, and beat Northern Area welterweight champion, Pat Hailey, who had to retire with a

Freddie Naylor in retirement with his scrapbooks.

badly cut eye in the first round of their fight. At Derby's Municipal Sports Ground, he also fought on the same bill as Empire heavyweight champion, Larry Gains.

After being raised in the uncompromising world of pre-war boxing, Naylor was always understandably cautious in his praise of modern boxers: "When I was fighting there were about 2,000 licensed professional boxers and I had about 350 fights. Now they seem to be getting title chances after only a few fights. I've had three 12-rounders in one week. And I once fought a man who fought three 12-rounders inside 24 hours. He was Siki Coulton, who fought on Saturday afternoon, Saturday evening, and Sunday afternoon."

Freddie Naylor retired from the ring at the age of 31, after beating a newly turned professional boxer from Wales: "It was the easiest £25 I ever earned. There was a terrific difference between seasoned pros and the top amateurs. I didn't win any medals or titles. But I fought with some great boxers and I thoroughly enjoyed my time in the ring."

After retiring from the police with the rank of sergeant, Freddie Naylor lived in retirement in Derby until his death.

Bar Was Set Low
For Derby Boys

O N EASTER Saturday 1946, 14-year-old Don Capenerhurst of Brighton Road School, and his pal, Pete Rowe, walked to the Baseball Ground with dreams of emulating Derby County. While the Rams were through to the FA Cup final – by coincidence that day they were playing Charlton Athletic, their Wembley opponents, in a League game in London – Don and his Derby Boys team-mates were getting ready to face Stockton Boys in the last eight of the English Schools Shield.

The town was buzzing with talk that Derby might achieve a unique football double – win the FA Cup and the schoolboy equivalent in the same season – and the young Capenerhurst's heart was pounding.

Before he retired to the Isle of Wight in 2010, Don recalled that moment: "I'll never forget that Saturday morning, my first game on the Baseball Ground. I walked from Alvaston with my teammate, Pete Rowe, and we hardly spoke a word. We approached the ground at the Osmaston End, past the bomb-damaged double-decker stand that had been hit in 1941, and then entered the ground by the main entrance in Shaftesbury Crescent.

"We'd arrived in plenty of time, to become accustomed to the strange atmosphere, because we'd never experienced anything like it. Derby Boys had won the Shield only once, in 1908, and here we were, hopefully on our way to repeat history. Of course, playing for Derby Boys in 1946 was very different from today. We left school at 14 and there was only one team, whereas now, almost every level seems to be represented and the minimum school leaving age is 16.

"The old leather footballs used to feel like cannonballs on a wet day, where today's footballs are always lightweight, no matter what the conditions. We had big heavy boots with leather studs – or cogs as we used to call them – and the referee inspected our boots before each game because the nails that held the cogs in had a nasty habit of sticking out. Of course, we had just 11 players and no subs, so if anyone got injured, you just had to soldier on with ten men."

Derby Boys in 1945-46. Left to right: Colgan (Pear Tree), Turner (Sinfin), R. Brown (Pear Tree), Robertson (Pear Tree), Capenerhurst (Brighton Road), Rowe (Brighton Road), Crossley (Kedleston Road), Curry (Central School), D. Brown (Pear Tree), Broadhurst (Derby School), Upton (Allenton).

"Our first game of 1945-46 was a friendly against Leicester Boys on Parker's Piece on City Road, where Derby School played. We lost 4-2, and then went to Oakwell on New Year's Day to play Barnsley Boys. They were a very strong side, but we won with a spectacular goal from Malcolm Curry of Central School, who scored with only five minutes to play.

"We had a good win in the first round of the English Schools Trophy, beating Ilkeston Boys 5-0, then we knocked out Nottingham Boys, 2-0 at Wollaton Park. That left us to face what the press were calling our strongest opponents yet, Grimsby Boys. But we beat them 8-0 at Normanton Barracks, so I don't know how they got that reputation. We were drawn at home again in the next round, against Sheffield Boys, and all 2,000 tickets were sold. The match was again held at Normanton Barracks and again we won. Their outside-right was a lad called Blenkinsop, whose father, Ernie, had played for Sheffield Wednesday and England."

Derby Boys were now in the quarter-finals, drawn away to Stockton Boys, Unusually, they travelled up the day before the match: "It was quite an experience. We stopped overnight in a hotel at Redcar. The game was played on the ground of the local Northern League club, but we had to change in a local school as the senior side were playing at home on the same pitch immediately after our game finished. When we ran out, we found the crowd were packed in right up to the touchline because 9,000 people had turned up and the ground was full to capacity.

"Under ESFA rules we had to use a lowered crossbar, which I could never understand because it was the same for both teams. Of course, the grounds we had been using until then just had a lower goal, but as this was a senior ground, they had to fasten another crossbar under the normal one. You wouldn't believe it, but we hit that lowered crossbar no less than three times in the course of the game. If they'd left the goal alone, we'd have won easily."

As it was, Derby Boys drew 1-1 to bring Stockton back for a replay. Now, however, Derby had a problem because interest in the game was so high that Normanton Barracks could not cope. The boys approached Derby County, who allowed them to use the Baseball Ground. So on Saturday, 20 April, 1946, Don Capenerhurst found himself walking into what was a local schoolboy's theatre of football dreams.

"I remember looking around the dressing-room and thinking about all the great players who had changed there – Steve Bloomer, Jack Bowers and Jack Barker, and what were then present-day heroes like Dally Duncan, Raich Carter and Peter Doherty. And I was fascinated by this great big bath, big enough for all the players to jump in at once. At Normanton Barracks, we had to share one sink. Normally, our dressing-room was full of laughter, but not this April morning. We were so nervous that the place was like a morgue. After our team talk, which consisted of nothing more than: 'Good luck lads'", we ran out to find a crowd of over 10,000. We expected a big attendance, but not that many."

And there the dream ended. Stockton went through, 2-1 after extra-time. "I'm sure that we'd have won if we'd played at the Barracks," says Don, "but on the day, the experience of playing at the Baseball Ground was alien to us." There was a treat in store for Derby's schoolboy footballers, however. They travelled to play Brighton Boys in the first leg of a challenge cup given by the officers and crew of the Royal Navy ship, HMS *Derbyshire*.

"We won 2-0 on Brighton and Hove Albion's ground. We were given a reception at the Royal Pavilion, a tour of the district and visited the theatre. On the way home we beat Leicester Boys – who won the ESFA Shield that season – 2-0 at Filbert Street. And we beat Brighton 8-4 in the return leg at the Baseball Ground."

The following season, the Derby Boys team was kept together to play in the Derby Welfare League. Strengthened by players like Jack Parry, who went on to play for the Rams, Tony Grogan and "Ginger" Clarke, they won Section D of the league with a remarkable record: played 19, won 18, goal scored 215, goals against 9. In one game, against Derby West End on Osmaston Park, Derby School Old Boys won 30-0.

Then Shelton United took the players on as a nursery for Derby County and Don was on amateur forms with the Rams for five years. Eventually National Service broke up the Shelton team and they all went their separate ways. In the meantime, the 1949 Derby Boys team, another excellent side, reached the Schools Shield final, where they lost to Barnsley. Don was at the game, cheering Derby on, and at the same time wondering how things might have worked out three years earlier, but for that lowered crossbar.

Derby and a Crowning Glory

I T WAS the crowning of Elizabeth II on Tuesday, 2 June 1953, that occupied almost everyone in Derby. By the end of May, the town's Coronation celebrations were well under way. The biggest in Derby – the Derby and County Coronation Year Exhibition – was held on Bass's Recreation Ground from 29 May until 13 June. Some 400 stands were erected, staffed by 1,500 people representing organisations and businesses of all descriptions, including Rolls-Royce and British Celanese, who presented their "Court of Fashion". This featured beautiful creations by top designers of the day, including Norman Hartnell, who, six years earlier, had designed the new queen's wedding dress, all made from Celanese fabrics. The exhibition enjoyed an average daily attendance of 7,000 and several local businesses reported making important overseas trading contacts.

Derbyshire had its own representatives in the official Coronation celebrations, too. Derby-born Constance Spry was commissioned to decorate Westminster Abbey for the ceremony and, with her creative and business partner, Rosemary Hume, invented a cold buffet dish – Coronation Chicken.

Littleover's Stan Bellaby, a 22-year-old lance-sergeant in the Queen's Company, Grenadier Guards, was one of those chosen to mount guard over the crown and coronation regalia. The former Derby Co-operative Society employee was due to be demobbed the following month, after five years' service in the Grenadiers and looked forward to joining Derbyshire County Police. Fifty years later, now retired from the police and living in Ripley, Stan Bellaby recalled that great day: "A temporary annex had been built on to Westminster Abbey, to be used by various dignitaries to get ready before entering the Abbey itself. We stood shoulder to shoulder around the edge of the room, with rifles and bayonets and no room to move. I recognised many faces from newspaper photographs. The one that still stick in my mind is Winston Churchill, who was within touching distance of me."

Another local man serving in the Grenadier Guards, 20-year-old Lawrence Lambert, whose family lived at Lord Street, Allenton, would be in the Coronation procession, and 21-old Musician Eric Beardsall, from Allen Street, Allenton, would be playing the euphonium in the Royal Naval School of Music Band in the procession, while yet another Derby representative would be 19-year-old Daniel Docherty of Brackens Lane, Alvaston, who was one of the Irish Guardsman chosen to line the route.

In Derby, official celebrations began the day before the Coronation, with schools closing at Monday lunchtime until Wednesday morning, the exception being the town's grammar schools where examinations meant that pupils would have only Coronation Day off. That Monday morning, some 23,000 Derby children received an inscribed spoon from the Education Authority and at each school an appropriate ceremony was held "to bring home to the children the meaning and significance of the Coronation". Meanwhile, the peace of the Riverside Gardens was broken by two loud explosions from across the Derwent, near Exeter flats, where armoured cars of the Derbyshire Yeomanry were practising the 21-gun salute they were due to give at 10.26am on Coronation Day, at the exact moment the Queen would leave Buckingham Palace on her way to Westminster Abbey.

The cold and damp Coronation Day weather did its best to bed-raggle the bright bunting that decorated most of the county's streets, but did little to dampen spirits. Those lucky enough to own televisions threw open their doors to neighbours, who gathered around the tiny, flickering black and white screens for hours on end. Many others saw the ceremony on televisions in a large tent at Bass's Rec.

The inclement weather conditions caused the cancellation of some events. The fireworks display at Markeaton Park was one –

a display held the previous Saturday had attracted 2,000 people who saw an image of the Queen's face surmounted by a crown outlined in white and yellow fireworks – while at Normanton Park, the Sherwood Foresters Band played as scheduled and the Middies managed a display of counter-marching before the rest of the programme was cancelled.

The fair at the Racecourse did a little better, with a steady stream of children enjoying the rides and sideshows, while local cricketers struggled gamely through their tournament in weather more suitable for football. Not surprisingly, considering that most of the exhibits were indoors, events on Bass's Rec attracted by far the most visitors.

In Derby there were nearly 250 street parties. The Town Council had allocated 12 guineas (£12.60) as prizes to be awarded to the three best-decorated streets in the borough. The residents of Grey Street, off Gerard Street, won first prize. Tubs containing masses of flowers were set at regular intervals on the pavements down either side of the street, every window sill had a window box filled with red, white and blue flowers, and at the bottom of the street, a large board proclaimed: "God Save The Queen," while naval signal flags spelled out the same message. The mayoress received a bouquet from five-year-old Valerie Wood, whose parents had organised the decorations and who themselves were presented with a "hall set" by grateful neighbours. Tewkesbury Street and Gisborne Street tied for second place, and there were commendations for Winchester Crescent, Colombo Street, Norman Street, Birdwood Street, Harcourt Street, St Luke's Street, York Street, Bath Street, Albion Street, Canal Street and Nelson Street.

Almost every street leading from London Road, between The Spot and Bateman Street, held a party, and many forms of alternative accommodation were negotiated in a bid to beat the elements as schoolrooms, garages, cycle sheds and the spare rooms behind pubs were utilised. Yates Street celebrated beneath a "God Save the Queen" banner some 116 years old; it had hung over the same street on Queen Victoria's Coronation Day in 1837.

While many parties were forced indoors because of the weather, 60 children from Osmaston Road refused to be daunted and donned raincoats to eat their tea in the open. In Harrison Street, too, scores of children ignored the rain and insisted on enjoying their tea in the street as planned. Residents of Underhill Avenue had also managed their tea and were about to embark on their sports when the rain came down again. There was a brief interval while mothers went to fetch raincoats and wellington boots, and then the festivities continued, although the participants in the ladies versus gents cricket match got thoroughly soaked. Many communities arranged their own fancy dress competition: in Etwall Street, one up-to-the-minute costume was that of a mountaineer, a tribute to the first successful attempt on Mount Everest, which had been announced earlier that day.

For several families. Coronation Day was marked by a new arrival. Mr and Mrs Geoffrey Ellis celebrated the birth of a baby son, while Mrs Kathleen Storer welcomed her daughter, Elizabeth June. Other Coronation Day babies included a daughter to Mrs Betty Jackson, born at home in Curzon Lane, Alvaston; Elizabeth Danuta Wasikowska and Jill Bennett were born at the Queen Mary Maternity Home, while six babies – Hans Peter Foss, Neville William Hollies, Sarah Sherbrook, Michael Robert Poole, Philip John Hunkin, and Donald William Holmes – were born at the Nightingale Maternity Home. At the City Hospital, one boy – Anthony John Dakin – and one girl – Elizabeth Mary Snuggs – also made their entrance.

Two weeks after the Coronation, there was an additional treat for 13,000 children from town and county who attended local cinemas to see film of the glorious event. The Gaumont on London Road showed both a newsreel and a 90-minute Technicolor film entitled *A Queen is Crowned*, which was narrated by Sir Laurence Olivier. Audiences at the Odeon in St Peter's Street and the Regal in East Street were treated to *Elizabeth is Queen*, a newsreel and a film about Westminster Abbey.

For many, the Coronation celebrations seemed to mark the end of post-war austerity in Britain and a new hope for the future. As the year drew to a close, the people of Derby looked forward, with enthusiasm to a new Elizabethan Age.

A Ration-Free Christmas

D ERBEIANS HAD been used to queuing and, to the casual observer, this Christmas Eve seemed no different. Slowly the line of people moved down Green Lane, shoulders hunched against the chill air. It was so reminiscent of all those dreary days spent shuffling along outside a shop, not always even knowing what was on offer at the end of it all. But this time it was different, The dateline on the copies carried by the *Derby Evening Telegraph* newspaper seller patrolling the queue gave the clue: it was December 24, 1954 – Derby's first ration-free Christmas for 14 years.

Those in line were not queuing for food. They were waiting to enter the Hippodrome theatre, where Stan Stennett and More-cambe and Wise were opening in the pantomime, *Babes in the Wood*.

For the first Christmas in the lifetimes of many Derby children, there was no need to worry about how many precious ration coupons had been saved up for these festivities. And for one young Derby boy, in particular, it was a special occasion. Nine-year-old Stuart Clay lived just around the corner from the Hippodrome, and his family provided lodgings for performers appearing at the theatre. Morecambe and Wise had stayed with the Clays before, even taking young Stuart and his brother and sister to the fair on Bass's Rec one afternoon. The young lad was already well acquainted with Eric and Ernie, later to become such a legendary comedy duo.

But Stuart, who later served as policeman in Derby for 34 years, also remembered that first Christmas as the time when ration books could be thrown away: "We'd grown up after the war, quite used to rationing. Sweets were just one of the items for which you needed coupons. Then everything came off ration and, after that, what you could buy was governed simply by what was available. Just round the corner from the Hippodrome, in Macklin Street, there was a shop run by an American called Joe Sherrin. I think he'd come over here as a serviceman during the war, and stayed on. He sold the best ice-cream in Derby, and this was the shop where we went with our sweet coupons, and to buy all our Christmas fare."

In 1954, Christmas in Derby was a truly family occasion – even if many sons would miss the celebrations because of National Service – and the Mayor of Derby, Alderman Alec Ling, told a Christmas Eve carol concert in the Market Place: "If Derby can maintain – or improve – its family atmosphere and structure, then its long record of prosperity will be outmatched by further progress."

Unlike today, the holiday lasted for only three days, and that only because Boxing Day fell on a Sunday, thus giving people an extra day off that weekend."

And as Derbeians made the most of the fact that they didn't need ration books, the shops were bustling all the previous week: "Derby goes on a £-million spending spree!" proclaimed the headline on that Christmas Eve edition of the *Evening Telegraph*. And at 1954 prices that must have been some spending spree: Ranbys advertised a string of pearls from 2s 11d (less than 15p) and handbags for less than £5. In the store's toy department, doting parents could buy their child a scooter for 13s (65p), a tricycle for less than £7, and large dolls from 16s (80p).

At John Manners, presents for the man of the house ranged from a quality shirt with detachable collar and cuffs for one guinea (£1.05) to dressing gowns at £2 15s (£2.75). And if a new carpet was on order for Christmas, Derby families could expect to pay two shillings (10p) a week for an Axminster or Wilton on hire purchase.

Turkey was 5s (25p) per pound, but one shopkeeper warned that tea would soon be a luxury item at 10s (50p) per pound. He blamed the shortage on the fact that Americans were now drinking more of our national beverage.

Perhaps the most telling comparison was that, half a century ago, a cigarette smoker would pay the equivalent of less than 7p for 10 Park Drive. And, of course, almost every one lit up. Every bus, pub, shop, cinema, and just about every home, was a fog of cigarette smoke.

For sports fans that Christmas, while Frank Tyson was bowling England to a 38-run win over Australia in the Second Test at Sydney, Derby County were plummeting into the Third Division North for the first time in their history.

A week before Christmas, the club's former England right-back, Bert Mozley, played his last game for the Rams – a 1-1 draw with Notts County at the Baseball Ground – before emigrating to Canada. Today Bert still lives there with his wife, Jean, in Victoria, British Columbia. He recalls that sad day: "My old pal, Leon Leuty, was their captain and as we shook hands at the end, they played *Auld Lang Syne* over the loudspeakers. I had a lump in my throat. In the stands, Jean had tears in her eyes. The fans gave me a great send off and I'll never forget that day as long as I live."

For non-sports fans there were 16 cinemas in Derby, including the Cavendish, Normanton and Spondon. The week after Christmas, Derby Playhouse in Sacheverel Street staged a production of *Vanity Fair*. For the town's dancers there were the Ritz and Trocadero ballrooms on Normanton Road, the old Assembly Rooms in the Market Place, and the Cinderella Rooms at the Churchill Hall in Curzon Street.

On 23 December, 1954, two young girls had a miraculous escape when an 80mph blew down a two-hundredweight pinnacle from St Alkmund's Church. The girls were asleep in a bedroom in Old Church House when the masonry just missed the roof on its way down.

At 3am on Christmas Day, two women had a narrow escape when they were rescued from a burning house in Yates Street after they had passed their sons, aged eight and three, to safety through a bedroom window. Only prompt action by Derby Borough Fire Brigade saved the adults too.

Derby's first new arrival on Christmas Day, 1954, was Christopher John Smith, who was born at Derby City Hospital just after midnight. Meanwhile, in Shaw Street, Mr and Mrs William Dumelow celebrated their golden wedding anniversary on Christmas Day, when Mr Dumelow told an *Evening Telegraph* reporter that he once played football with the great Steve Bloomer. On Christmas Day afternoon, the Queen gave her traditional broadcast over the wireless. Listeners also enjoyed programmes from the golden age of radio comedy: *Life With The Lyons*, *A Life Of Bliss* and *Take It From Here*.

And as Bert and Jean Mozley looked forward to a new life on other side of the Atlantic, young Stuart Clay tucked into his Christmas dinner and relished a future without sweet rationing.

Market Hall Memories

IT WAS the place where the first-ever bananas to arrive in Derby were put on sale, where literally hundreds of rabbits were once sold each week for Derbeians' rabbit pie, and where Derby's 19th-century police officers train in its cobbled yard. At a time when we've become accustomed to shopping almost around the clock, and when the giant Westfield Derby now attracts hundreds of thousands of people to the city centre – some may argue that Westfield actually attracts folk away from the proper city centre – it's interesting to muse that, around the turn of the last century, this Derby trading institution thought nothing of a 17-hour day. Another, unlike the cosy, dry Westfield shopping experience, conditions here were often draughty and bitterly cold.

It's 35 years ago since the demolition of the old fish market, in what is now Osnabruck Square, opposite the *Derby Telegraph's* former home in the green-domed Corn Exchange building, gave Derbeians a new view of one of the city's great old favourites – the Market Hall. Love it or hate it – most love it but there a few locals who do not feel comfortable there – Derby Market Hall enjoys an undeniably unique atmosphere with its echoing acoustics, and its comparatively spartan conditions, all of which add a great deal of character to one of the city's most cherished shopping areas. Sadly, of course, some of the stalls are now empty as shopping habits change.

In a city that has changed so much over the past quarter of a century – and that change is now taking place at a whirlwind pace – the Market Hall, is probably the last major link with the disappearing Derby of other generations. One would like to say that it's still bustling and noisy, but, in fact, even that is becoming

91

muted as the 21st century gets well under way. The roof has been known to leak – come to think of it, so has that of the spanking-new Westfield – but in these times of supermarkets, hypermarkets, plush department stores and American-style shopping malls, the Market Hall offers a nostalgic trip into another shopping age – and that is meant as a compliment.

Derby Market Hall was built in 1864-5 at a cost of £29,000, with its decorated cast-iron columns, glazed roof and ornate clock, which told the time to generations of Derbeians anxious to catch a tram or a train, or in later years, when the time was up on their parked cars.

In those early days there were two rows of flower stalls near the Cornmarket, and a row of wholesale stalls, while the fish market ran along the side of the Market Place. There it remained until a new fish market was erected on the south side of the Market Place in 1926. It was the demolition of that building in the early 1980s that allowed us to view the Market Hall as it had looked before the First World War.

The first Jamaican bananas in Derby were sold in the Market Hall. Until the end of the 19th century, bananas grown on the plantations of the Caribbean and elsewhere were solely for use there, until businessmen became alive the possibilities of exporting them to Europe. It wasn't then long before Derbeians were able to enjoy this new exotic fruit.

At the beginning of the 20th century, Market Hall stallholders worked very long hours – from 6am to 11pm on Saturdays, for instance – and the hall closed on only two days each year – Christmas Day and Good Friday.

When Derby County played big FA Cup-ties in the days of Steve Bloomer, and when the crowds flocked to Derby races on Nottingham Road, the Market Hall staged penny bazaars in the gallery that surrounded the inner area. These were the days of an open market in the Market Place, of rich customers in carriages, of barrow boys, and of gas lamps casting their eerie glow in the colonnade underneath the Guildhall Then there was the cold. In those days, the Market Hall had no doors and eventually a deputation went to see the Markets Committee. The stallholders got their doors, and also won a promise that the Market Hall would be repainted and refitted.

Adjacent to the Market Hall, in the Lock-Up Yard – where the fish market (and also a monument to the great Steve Bloomer) is now sited – was a police station. The policemen of Victorian Derby were often seen doing their physical jerks in the cobbled yard that ran from the Cornmarket past the lock-up and into the Market Hall. In that lock-up was kept something known as "the stretcher", although it looked more like a shallow coffin complete with straps. The policemen used it to tame unruly prisoners, usually drunks, although Market Hall stallholders occasionally used it to carry their goods to storage in the Morledge.

In 2004, Jean Wacey, by then living in British Columbia, wrote to the *Derby Telegraph* with memories of her first job when she left school – working on a stall in Derby Market Hall in 1938. Jean earned 7s (40p) for a 48-hour week. "About standard for the time," she recalled.

In fact, the interior of the Market Hall was completely reconstructed in 1938, and the roof was completely recovered in 1964, although the essential character remained largely unchanged since Thorburn's original design of almost 150 years ago. In 1989, another refurbishment restored the Victorian design, so, ironically, many of today's Derbeians, at least those over 25, have lost "their" Market Hall interior, which was of pre-war rather than 19th-century design.

At the time of its opening, the Market Hall housed 180 stalls on the ground floor and the balcony.

A Derby Corporation publication of the mid-1950s announced that the Market Hall housed 31 butchers and provision merchants, two caterers, 17 fruiterers, 10 florists, 55 newsagents, draper, china stores and their like, eight fish merchants, seven poulterers and livestock merchants. It had, the book said, "a splendid system of heating" and a "one-span roof, two-thirds allowing maximum natural daylight. During those years, and before, premises adjoining the poultry market housed live poultry, rabbits, dogs, cats, aquarium fish and a host of other pets. All these – fish market, poultry market and pet stores – were included in the wider term "covered market". But it is for the Market Hall itself that we feel most affection.

Speaking in 2004, a Derby City council spokesman said: "Today's Market Hall is a major attraction to the city and brings in visitors and shoppers from throughout this country. With traders who, for generations, have served the citizens of Derby and built up close links with their customers, are the new generation of traders bringing their own modern goods and ideas to the Hall.

"Separate fish and poultry sections and a large number of meat and fruit and vegetable traders ensure that the Hall gives the supermarkets a run for their money. Produce is fresh daily and many an office worker can find their lunches in the café's and stalls in the Hall. The Market Hall has adapted to the needs of the population, and together with newsagents, confectionary and clothing stalls, there has been the growth of service stalls, such as key-cutting, shoe repair, hairdressing, nail bar, and advice centres. Traders believe that the Market Hall is more than adequately equipped to evolve as the public becomes more demanding over the next decades, and that they the traders will rise to the challenge. There are craft stalls

Irongate in the 1950s. Today, the area isn't so busy with traffic but still thrives as part of the Cathedral Quarter.

available to let on a daily basis on the balcony with goods such as hand made items and antiques and bric-a-brac for sale."

In 2013, the picture is less rosy and Derby Market Hall is one of the final links with the town of yesterday. Today, with the advent of Westfield, the traditional shopping area has moved towards that giant shopping mall on the south side of the city centre, leaving some shop premises vacant. Victoria Street in particular looks a shadow of its former bustling self. So it is good to see the Cathedral Quarter, as that end of Derby has been rebranded, fighting hard to survive and, indeed, prosper.

A Far From Misspent Youth

T HE THEORY that a talent for billiards or snooker is the sign of a misspent youth was always quickly dispelled in the company of Derby's Herbert Beetham. A former world amateur billiards champion, three times English title holder, and, for decades, one of the greatest names in the game, his pedigree belied the stereotype of such a champion.

The silver-haired Beetham found his passion for the game, not in the seedy, smoke-filled twilight of pre-war billiards halls, but in the quiet sobriety of St Thomas's Church Institute in Pear Tree. Not only that, he managed to combine a world-class career as a billiards player with that of a successful businessman. For many years, he ran White's Brothers soft drinks company in Derby. His birthplace, 80 Havelock Road, was the factory house of that family business.

Herbert Beetham died in April 1992, at the age of 82. A couple of years earlier, he told me about his remarkable career, especially about the day he won the world title in Edinburgh, almost 30 years before.

"At first, it didn't seem real. But then I realised I was the world champion. It was the climax of 27 years' dedication from the time I first entered the English championship in 1932-33."

He was quick to dispel the theory that the success was at the expense of his schooling: "I've been asked about it many times. But I didn't start playing billiards seriously until I was 19. By then, of course, I'd finished grammar school, so the old chestnut about a misspent youth doesn't come into it. None of the family was involved in sport, although my father was interested in billiards. I'd first played a little bit on a small table and soon discovered that I had a natural ability for the game. Then I went on to play at St Thomas's Church Institute.

"In 1932, I entered the English championships and three years later, I reached the final. I lost by 30 points, and I could quite easily have won. But there is terrific pressure when you've got that far, and I was nervous."

Beetham reached the final again in 1946, and again he lost. He appeared in the 1952 and 1959 finals, and yet again finished runner-up. Then, in 1960, he took the title for the first time: "The previous year, Leslie Driffield beat me in the final. In 1960, Reg Wright of

Derby-born billiards champion Herbert Beetham
shows off his many trophies.

Leicestershire knocked out Leslie in the semi-final, and I met Reg in the final. After losing four English finals, I was determined to win the title at the fifth attempt. Sure enough, I defeated Reg and it was a wonderful moment in my life."

But if March 1960 was a highspot in Herbert Beetham's career, there was an even greater triumph just six months later, when he travelled to Edinburgh in a bid to become the first English world champion since Driffield's victory in Calcutta in 1952: "As it was held in Edinburgh, we decided to make it our family summer holiday that year. There were eight finalists, and we played each other on a league basis. My last opponent was W. J. Dennison of Ireland, and this is where there was a little bit of irony. Mr Dennison and I stopped at the same hotel and we looked around for a table on which to practise. We found one in a local snooker hall, and he beat me a couple of times.

"Of course, when we met in the world final, we knew each other's game. At one point, I was 100 points down, but I pulled it back to win by 1,173 points to 845. Again, there are no words to truly express my feelings. When you realise that you are the best in the world at your chosen sport, it's a wonderful thing."

Beetham retained his English title in 1961. The following year, he was invited to defend his world crown in Perth, Western Australia, but could not prevent Australia's Robert Marshall from taking the title for a record fourth time In 1963, Herbert won his third and final English title, and two years later he bowed out of the Derby Institutes League.

"I played for St Thomas's until 1960, when they disbanded, and then I joined the Wallbrook Institute. The best player at St Thomas's was a chap called Fred Minskip. I used to take every opportunity of playing with him and learning from him. I've always tried to play with better players. You can only improve that way."

He continued in the local knockout event for many more years, as a member of the Beaconsfield Club in Green Lane, and in 1977 reached another English final. There was one incident that still raised a smile. It came in a match he was playing against a Southampton undertaker.

"He dashed around the table, looking anything but an undertaker.

Eventually, he told me he was worried about his son. He'd left him in charge of a big military funeral and was more concerned about how the lad was doing than about the billiards."

Was he ever tempted to turn professional? "No, because, although I was always dedicated, billiards was my hobby, I never wanted it to become my job. Of course, I was fortunate because I had my business. I must have spent hundreds of pounds travelling to play billiards as an amateur. Perhaps in different circumstances, I wouldn't have had that opportunity, and then professionalism would have been a different matter. But, having said that, I am a big believer that when money comes in through the door, sportsmanship goes out through the window."

Herbert was a founder member and the first president of the Derbyshire Billiards and Snooker Association, and was Derbyshire's representative on the Billiards and Snooker Control Council. His funeral was attended by a great crowd of old friends, including many representatives of the world of billiards, and one tribute in the trade press summed him up: "Herbert Beetham achieved great things in the world of billiards – he became a champion. He achieved even greater things in the wider world – he became a much-loved man. No gathering of billiards enthusiasts was complete without Herbert Beetham's kindly presence. Something in all of us has died with him."

Flying Schoolteacher Footballer

NEWS THAT the president of Real Madrid valued David Beckham so highly that he was prepared to lay on a private jet to fly the England star to matches didn't surprise anyone in the crazy modern world of football extravagance. But 50 years earlier, there were plenty of raised eyebrows when the owner of Lincolnshire minnows, Boston United, provided an aircraft to fly Derby schoolteacher, Ray Wilkins, to play for his team in the old Midland League.

In the summer of 2005, Ray, who was then living in East Avenue, Mickleover, looked back over half a century to the days when, despite being a part-time footballer throughout a career which also saw him play for Derby County, he was considered such a valuable asset that his chairman would come calling in an aeroplane.

He recalled: "Boston was owned by the Malkinson family, who also owned entertainment venues along the East Coast. The chairman, Ernest Malkinson, was desperate to compete with Peterborough United, who in those days were the real East Anglian giants of non-League football. For instance, Peterborough had two ex-League goalkeepers as player-manager, Jack Fairbrother of Newcastle United, who was born in Burton, who was followed by George Swindin of Arsenal. So Mr Malkinson decided Boston should have one too. That led to him signing up Ray Middleton, Derby's former goalkeeper, as player-manager. And, in turn, Ray took several ex-Rams players, including me, to play for Boston."

For Ray Wilkins it was a chance to extend a professional playing career that had begun in whirlwind fashion: "I was studying at

Loughborough College, having just come out of the Royal Navy after three years compulsory service at the end of the Second World War. I played a couple of games for Moira United in the Christmas holidays of 1949 when Jack Nicholas, who was Derby's captain when they won the FA Cup in 1946, asked me to go for a trial at the Baseball Ground. To my astonishment, the next time I heard from Derby was to say that I was playing for the Reserves at Burnley. I hadn't even had the trial. Then things moved even faster. After only a couple of Reserves matches, I was in the first team against Liverpool.

"Jack Stamps was injured and I suddenly found myself playing centre-forward between two world-class inside-forwards, Johnny Morris and Billy Steel. Years later, after my mother died, we were clearing out her house and I found she'd kept all my old school exercise books. I was flicking through them one day and came across an entry I'd made in my English book in 1938. It read: 'One day I shall be a professional footballer and my team will be Derby County. I hope I shall score lots of goals.'" Ray couldn't remember writing those words, but they were certainly far-sighted, even down to scoring those goals: 11 in 30 games for the Rams alone would be a fair return in any era.

Ray was born in the South Derbyshire mining community of Albert Village in August 1928. When he was a year old, the family moved to Swadlincote, where Ray eventually went to Hastings Road Infants and Junior Schools. Then a scholarship took him to Ashby Grammar School, from where he went into the Navy, then to Loughborough.

Throughout a professional football career that took him to Derby, Boston, Wrexham, Oswestry Town and Macclesfield Town, he remained a part-time player, with teaching posts at Derwent and Sturgess Senior Schools in Derby, and St David's, a brand-new school in Wrexham, where he went back into League football with the Third Division club. "We would have stayed in Wrexham, but my first wife became very ill and we had to come back, so that her mother could help care for her."

Back in Derby, Ray became head of PE at Mackworth School, and played for local clubs, Gresley Rovers, Wilmorton and

Derby schoolteacher Ray Wilkins shakes hands with Boston United
chairman Ernest Malkinson at Burnaston in September 1954. Malkinson
has just sent a chartered an aircraft to take Wilkins and another Derby-
based player, Peter Wheatley (carrying bag), to Boston for a Midland
League match against Rotherham United Reserves.

Alvaston, and later managed Crewton FC. He went on to become head of the fifth year at Mackworth, and later senior teacher – effectively a deputy head – before retiring after the school became a comprehensive in the education upheaval of the 1970s.

He said: "I had long decided that when I was in my mid-40s, I would give up teaching PE and concentrate on academic subjects. I didn't want to end up like my old PE teacher at Ashby Grammar, who, because of the war and the shortage of young teachers, had to carry on well past the point where he could perform. It wasn't his fault, but I didn't want to end up the same."

When Ray assessed his football career, there was one memory that stood out above all others. In December 1955, Boston United came to the Baseball Ground to play Derby County in the FA Cup, with six ex-Rams players, including Ray and 1946 Cup winner, Reg Harrison, in their ranks. In one of the greatest Cup upsets of all time, Boston won 6-1 with ex-Rams reserve player, Geoff Hazledine, scoring a hat-trick. That morning Ray had been the subject of a newspaper article which had the schoolteacher-footballer claiming that Boston "would teach Derby a lesson".

Said Ray: "It was all tongue in cheek. We never expected to win, although we didn't expect to do badly either. Our plan was to play good football and show supporters of the club that had sacked us that we were still decent players. The result was beyond our wildest dreams. About an hour after the final whistle, Reg Harrison and myself decided to pay our respects to our former colleagues. We went into the Derby dressing-room and stopped in our tracks. The players still hadn't changed out of their kit and it was deadly silent. Harry Storer, the Derby manager, just swung round and glared at us. We retreated, closed the door gently, and tip-toed back down the corridor."

Another of Ray's memories was the startlingly different temperaments of Johnny Morris and Billy Steel, Derby's two British record signings of the late 1940s: "Johnny, who came from Manchester United and was an England international, was absolutely wonderful. He couldn't have been more helpful to a young player just starting out. He was always taking you to one side, offering advice.

"Billy, who'd played for Scotland and Great Britain, was just the opposite. He wanted the ball to his feet and wouldn't move a yard for it. If you gave him a less than perfect pass, he'd just let the ball go by, and shrug at the crowd as if to say, 'Did you see that? What a poor pass.' A lot of the senior players resented him because, in those days of a maximum wage for footballers, Derby found him a 'job' at Bennett's, thanks to one of the directors. They also got him a company car when others were still catching the bus."

At the time I interviewed him, Ray still attended every home game at Pride Park, and was an enthusiastic supporter of the Derby County Former Players' Association, and a keen golfer. He said: "I love Derby County and just wish they'd get back to the top where they belong." Until then, the chances of a private aircraft to ferry the occasional player about, are remote indeed.

A Real Life Boys' Own Hero

A WHIRLWIND 91 in only your second first-class cricket match, followed, two games later, by a bowling performance of eight for 54 which wrecked the opposition, are the sort of performances usually reserved for the more fanciful realms of sporting fiction. Couple it all with the fact that the cricketer in question was an amateur, a dashing ex-public schoolboy brimful of true Corinthian spirit and you have makings of a real-life boys' comic hero in the mould of the best that the *Wizard* or the *Hotspur* ever produced.

Yet they were the real-life exploits of a young man who burst upon the Derbyshire scene in the scorching summer of 1959, when 21-year-old William Richardson, lately of Winchester School and the Royal Artillery, found himself pitched into the county side when Harold Rhodes was playing for England. Forty-five years later, William was living in Quarndon and contenting himself with walking his dogs and watching local cricket, when he shared with me his memories of those golden days with Derbyshire.

The Richardsons are one of the Derbyshire's oldest families who can trace their roots back to the 17th century when they were farming at Horsley.

They became involved in the tanning industry and in 1624, one of William's forebears founded the family firm that traded for the next 360 years. Richardson's tanners eventually moved into Eagle Street but that works burned down in 1924, and the business then transferred to Sinfin Lane, where it stayed until folding in 1984.

"We were the fourth oldest company in the entire country and it was more than just a practical blow when we went under," William said. "Losing a family company, which had such a long and distinguished history, was hard to take, especially since it was caused by a production problem which should have been avoided. It was a very emotional time all round, however, because my father had died the previous year, and my mother died the following year.

It was William's father who began the family's cricketing tradition. Arthur Walker Richardson, who was born in Quarndon, was 29 when in 1936, as an amateur, he skippered Derbyshire to the only County Championship title in the club's history. In the early 1990s, William's son, Alastair, carried on the family tradition by appearing in two first-class matches for Derbyshire.

When William started his county career, amateur cricketers were "gentlemen" and enjoyed the distinction of having their initials *before* their surname. There is the story of an announcement at Lord's that boomed out on the first morning of a Middlesex match: "Please note that on the scorecard, F.J. Titmus should read Titmus F.J." The off-spinner might have been good enough to play for England but as far as Lord's were concerned, he was only a common professional.

But there were more significant differences between the current county game and the one that the young Richardson had played over 40 summers before. In those days, almost everybody, whether they were paid or not, seemed to play for fun.

"I remember that knock of 91 against Glamorgan very well. When I got to the middle, George Dawkes, our wicketkeeper, was batting at the other end and the pitch was a typical Swansea turner. I asked George what I should do and he just said: 'Hit it!' So I did."

In fact William Richardson hit it exceedingly hard on that May afternoon. By tea he had plundered the Glamorgan attack for 91 in 92 minutes – in those day innings were measured in time not balls received – and his haul including four sixes and 13 fours.

"It was my own fault that I didn't get a century. I needed eight runs in five minutes to beat the season's fastest century, which I knew had been scored earlier that day. I missed a straight half-volley from their great captain, Wilf Wooller, and that was that." William

*Derbyshire CCC in 1962. William Richardson
is third from the left on the front row.*

and Bob Berry, Derbyshire former England left-arm spinner, added 81 runs for nine wickets that afternoon. Berry's contribution was just six runs.

William's fourth match was against Kent at Chesterfield and, coming on as first change, he took eight wickets for 54 runs with his erratic left-arm pace bowling as Kent tumbled to an innings defeat. His victims included England's Colin Cowdrey.

"I can't say I used any guile. I wasn't the straightest bowler in the world, but my theory was that if I didn't know where the ball was going, then the batsmen wouldn't have a clue either. The only man to suffer was probably George Dawkes behind the stumps, although he was a fine wicketkeeper and in that match against Kent he caught three off me."

Kent had every reason to rue the sight of G. W. Richardson in 1959. Later that summer he took seven for 31 at Canterbury to help Derbyshire to a 99-run victory. Again Cowdrey was one of his victims, caught by the Derby County footballer, Ian Hall. William played for Derbyshire until 1965, scoring 1,206 runs at an average of 14.88 and taking 134 wickets and the then respectable average of 27.10 runs apiece. But by the time he had played his last game, the seeds were already being sown for today's intensely commercial product in its many guises.

"When I started out, we all played for fun. I know I was an amateur who didn't depend on the game for a living, but even the professionals went out to enjoy themselves. Today, the pressures brought by the financial rewards available have spoiled the game. In my early days there were some greats characters, both players and umpires. Fred Trueman was a marvellous chap. They used to say he 'conned' about 30 wickets a season. Not cheating, please understand, nor gamesmanship like we say today, but pure kidology I suppose you'd call it.

"We had an opening batsman called Ray Swallow, who'd also played soccer for Arsenal and Derby County, by the way. One day Fred came into our dressing-room and demanded: 'Which one of you is Swallow?'

"When Ray introduced himself, Fred said: 'I understand you fancy yourself as a bit of a hooker – well you'd better watch out if you try any of that stuff today.' Ray expected the first ball he received from Fred to be short. He was already on the back foot when Fred let go with a beauty of a yorker. Ray had been conned, you see, but it was all fair and above board."

According to William, the pressures began with the Gillette Cup, cricket's first one-day knockout competition: "We were playing at Northampton on FA Cup Final day in 1964 and Ian Hall, who also played for the Rams, made a superb diving stop in the field. I called over: 'Come on Ian, you're not at Wembley today!' No one laughed and I got a rollicking from the skipper, Charlie Lee, who was a real dour professional.

"I'm glad I played when I did. I'd be out on my ear if I played today. The game is all about containment – and I never bowled straight enough for that."

William remembered the old Scarborough cricket festivals with great affection: "They were tremendous fun. I played for the Gentlemen against the Players, for Tom Pearce's team against the tourists, and for MCC against Yorkshire. Sadly, all that has gone. I was very fortunate to play against some fine cricketers like Peter May, Colin Cowdrey, Tom Graveney, Alec Bedser, Frank Tyson and Fred Trueman. Hampshire's skipper Colin Ingleby-Mackenzie was also a fine cricketer and very underrated.

"I remember seeing Brian Statham bowl a rare bouncer at Derby. The Lancashire wicketkeeper couldn't do a thing about it and it went for six byes. We all fell about laughing – and there's the difference; you wouldn't see anybody smiling about that today. Another odd thing is all this warming up and warming down that players do. We never trained, we just practised cricket. I once told our coach, Denis Smith, that my leg muscles were stiff. He just sucked on his pipe and said: 'Well, lad, what brought it on will take it off.'

"Les Jackson, our great opening bowler, must have bowled about 2,000 overs a season and I don't remember him missing a game through injury. Nowadays they have all these so-called sports drinks. I don't know what Les would make of that. At the end of a hot day's play, we each had a pint of beer waiting for us in the dressing-room.

"Of course, I can't say if modern cricketers really enjoy the game because I'm not involved any more. All I know is that I don't enjoy watching the one-day stuff with floodlights, coloured clothing and music. I'll watch Test matches on the television but I haven't seen Derbyshire play for several years now. I prefer to go up the road to watch Quarndon. There are some jolly fine players in local cricket."

Then it was time to walk the dogs – around Quarndon cricket ground, of course.

Memories of a Derby Hairdresser

PHIL VIDOFSKY'S barber's shop in Abbey Street was my unsentimental introduction to a grown-up's world. Every fortnight in the late 1940s and through the 1950s I was sent there for a trim and a dollop of Brylcreem.

It was more than just a place where hair was cut. It was a social club where, each day, the same old men would congregate – whether they needed a haircut or not – and gossip with Phil and whoever was in his chair, while his wife kept everyone supplied with huge cups of steaming tea. I was fascinated watching Phil singe hair with lighted wax tapers, and lather men's faces before shaving them with a cut-throat razor that he kept sharp by stropping on a leather belt.

While you waited your turn, there were *Tom Mix* comics to read, men were discreetly asked: "Anything for the weekend, sir?" and Phil sold Nemo's football sweep tickets and took illegal bets that he passed on to a bookie's runner who transferred them to a back-street turf accountant at the top of Wilson Street. He also chain smoked, lighting one cigarette from another and blowing smoke over you as he snipped away. My greatest day there came was I was big enough for Phil to dispense with the board that he set across the arms of the barber's chair for junior clients.

In the mid-1950s, Derby Town Council told Phil that his shop was in the way of Derby's planned inner ring road. So he left for London. He returned five years later, opened another hairdresser's, in Harry Thurman's old tobacconist's shop at the junction of Wilson Street and Gerard Street – in a direct line with his old one – ran it for 20 years, and then enjoyed a decent retirement, still waiting for the council to start work on that bit of the inner ring road.

Phil was an East End Jew of Polish descent, born in the Commercial Road. His parents had moved to Derby before the First World War, to live in the Little City, that rabbit warren of narrow streets off Burton Road, their names – Cannon Street, Trafalgar Street and so on – bearing testament to their origins during the Napoleonic wars. Phil's wife, Gladys, was also Jewish, a Cohen by birth. But she was universally known as Bubbles because she'd been the baby of the family.

I caught up with Phil again on a mellow September afternoon in 1979, a few days after he'd retired. "I remember your mother first bringing you in for a hair cut when you were about two," he said. It was just after the end of the war. You screamed the place down."

For the past few years, Phil had been a fervent campaigner for the speedy rehousing of Abbey Street area folk. Now it had caught up with him personally. Had he any regrets? "No regrets, but, now it's here, it's come as a bit of shock," he said. After all, I've lived for all but five years of my life in this area. This shop is just a couple of hundred yards from my first home in Derby."

Phil had learned his trade with a seven-year apprenticeship at Harry Murdock's shop in Abbey Street before branching out on his own just before the start of the Second World War.

"Harry Murdock gave me one piece of golden advice: 'You'll hear everyone else's trouble and ills. But never tell 'em your own.' It's something that I've never forgotten. And the shop's been more like a club than a business. Bubbles brewed up tea in the back for customers and the atmosphere has been wonderful. It's a dying part of city life, which is a pity, because I honestly feel that we were performing a social service as well as just cutting hair.

"I always set aside a day to visit sick customers and I've even lain under a bed at the DRI to cut the hair of a chap which was flat on his back in a plaster cast.

"We used to wax men's moustaches – that was a big part of the trade – but then that died out, and so too did the old short-back-and-sides. Men were coming out of the forces and they wanted to grow their hair longer and forget that horrible army haircut."

On this early autumn day, he and Bubbles were still living at the Gerard Street premises, but the door was now locked, the "Sorry, We're Closed" sign turned for the last time. We sat in the now deserted shop. A low sun shone through the window, reflecting off the big mirror that dominated one wall. Scissors and combs were still in their pots, an electric hair-trimmer still plugged in. But there were going to be no more customers. Was he sad?

"Not sad. I've enjoyed what I called the bread-and-butter-side of the trade. I've met a lot of wonderful people and a lot of interesting characters and, of course, I'm going to miss them. But I hope they'll still come and see us when we move."

Phil and Bubbles enjoyed a happy retirement in Churchside Walk, in the shadow of St Luke's Church, although it could have been longer. Phil was 78 when he died in July 1990. Bubbles died three years later. I doubt that we shall see their like again.

Painful Parting for Popular Apothecary

SINCE 1879, generations of Derbeians had entered the fascinating world of Ashley's chemists on Cheapside. They went to have their colds eased, their wounds dressed, and foreign bodies removed from their eyes. Even pets and farm animals had received medical treatment both from the old-time apothecary and the modern-day chemist at the old building that stood in the shadow of St Werburgh's church.

Now, in December 1980, the present proprietor, Jack Brittain, was ending almost half a century of tending to the aches and pains of Derby folk, many of whom he'd come to regard as friends rather than simply as customers. I'd worked with Jack Brittain's son, Roger, and when he alerted me to the fact that his father was about to retire, I had to talk to him.

The building, in itself worthy of a visit, pre-dated the chemist's business that was started as Brooks's grocer and apothecary in the final years of the 18th century. Eventually Mr Brooks took a partner, Mr Ashley, and it was for the fourth generation Ashley – Edmund – that Jack Brittain had come to work in 1933: "He was a grand boss and very well-known in theatrical circles in Derby, particularly for Gilbert and Sullivan."

The Ashleys lived in accommodation over the shop and Jack Brittain remembered that they had a housemaid and a servant boy. When Jack announced his intention to marry his girlfriend, Marjorie, the couple were invited to take tea with the Ashleys, with the attendant ringing of bells for the servants to wait upon them.

Eventually, the male line of the Ashley's dwindled and Jack Brittain took over the running of the business, himself soon becoming a familiar figure in Derby, known as a kind and knowledgeable man, always ready to give advice and assistance to anyone in need. The shop itself was something of a museum and Jack showed me a box of fearsome-looking pliers and pincers once used for extracting teeth. What anaesthetic was used? "None. The patient just used to grab hold of the chair arms and hold on. Don't worry. I'm not allowed to take out teeth these days."

Another fascinating reminder of the days of the old apothecary was a black tin with small air holes punched in the top. It was used for keeping leeches: "They would be sold to someone who perhaps sported a black eye. The idea was for the leech to take hold and then start sucking out the blood. It was then removed and there was something in its saliva that prevented the blood from coagulating and the bruise would drain. You'd then put the leech in salt to make it vomit, and then it went back in the box, ready to use all over again." One item for which Jack Brittain was still asked, even in 1980, was "five penn'orth", something that had been passed down from generation to generation: "People still ask me for this which was, quite literally, a mixture of five different ha-porths [halfpennies] with which we used to treat coughs. It consisted of a ha-porth each of oil of almonds, syrup of violets, syrup of tolu, syrup of ipecac, and syrup of squill."

Despite the fact that he was still occasionally asked for this concoction, Jack felt that self-medication was a dying art that would lead to the demise of many of the old type of chemist's shops: "People tend to go straight to the doctor's, these days, whereas at one time they would come to see us. Of course, we had to be careful about prescribing medicine for folk. This isn't, and never has been, a surgery."

At one time, Jack made all his own pills: "Every Monday morning was spent with the pill-making machine and I think I'm right in saying that, once we close, there'll be no chemist left in Derby who can do that."

What about those mysterious coloured bottles that was the trademark feature of all chemists' shops? "The old apothecary used them for making his own preparations and the leaf or bark of certain plants was left to dissolve on shelves in the window. The process was modernised but the bottles became a feature, filled up with coloured water and displayed on shelves in the windows." He also showed me a jar of what looked like chocolate drops but which turned out to be for easing canine coughs. In the past, everything from chickens and horses to the proverbial sick parrot had been treated on the Cheapside premises.

"The days of the old-time chemist are numbered. Everybody just wants a quick turnover. If it isn't a brand product advertised on television then most chemist's don't find it popular and so they won't stock it." Just then the shop bell rang and a man appeared at the counter, asking for two ounces of flowers of sulphur: "I've been everywhere in Derby ... "

Freedom to Roam

WHEN I was at Bemrose School there was a sixth former called Bob Wilson (his twin brother, Bill, was also at the school) who seemed to inspire the best in most people (alas, not always me, though; he once told me how disappointed he was that I'd skived off the house cross-country championships because of an alleged heavy cold). Bob Wilson was one of those irritating youths: good at everything. Football, cricket, athletics, music, and drama – he threw himself into it all with a vengeance. I bet if they'd entered him for the Grand National and the Boat Race as well, he would have jumped at the chance. In the time that our paths intertwined at Bemrose, he was both my house captain – Newton House – and the school captain. I never forgave him for telling me to go in goal in the first-ever house football trial in which I took part. I protested that I had never played in goal in my life, but he countered with the argument that I was the tallest player in the team. I argued back and although I lost, I ultimately made my point. We lost 13-0. And that wasn't because I wasn't trying. Anyway, almost 60 years later, our paths collided again. And now I have forgiven Robert Wilson, as he is now known. Not least because he responded to my plea for a contribution to this book with the following delightful account of his earliest years:

"BORN IN DERBY in November 1939, for my first six years I was surrounded by the trappings of war: uniformed personnel, anti-aircraft guns, searchlights, barrage balloons, air raid sirens, and even the bombed erstwhile home of my aunt's parents nearby. But I never twigged there was a war on. Many of its jigsaw pieces were there, but I failed to make the connections and complete the

115

picture, despite an RAF officer being billeted with us, my twin brother Bill and I often sleeping in a cubby hole under the stairs, and Dad replacing his budgerigar aviary in our garden with a solid brick air raid shelter, complete with bunk beds.

"For me, peace produced a precious freedom to roam, made possible by my having not only trusting parents but also a dependable twin brother to accompany me. Bikeless, our 'roaming territory' was constrained only by our willingness to walk or our reluctance to spend precious pocket money on bus rides. Some ramblings took us three or four miles from home – perhaps to semi-derelict Stenson Bubble, or bustling Burnaston aerodrome – but many were more local, often to the same places out of necessity or pleasure.

"We walked unescorted to primary school. We lived in Littleover Lane, Old Normanton, but attended St Peter's C of E School, Littleover, a half-hour's carefree dawdle away down our lane and up Normanton Lane, garnering other children en route. Almost no cars to contend with, just the occasional cyclist. Forty-eight children in our class at one stage, sitting in single desks usually in alphabetical order by surname. In our time there, the school closed just once, in early 1947. Extreme cold plus a fuel shortage froze up the inkwells, rendering our dip pens unusable. Until that point we had carried on, wearing overcoats all day if necessary.

"Like many others, Bill and I had school dinners. They were cooked elsewhere, and senior lads (working in pairs, with one handle each) took daily turns at lugging heavy shiny metal containers from the delivery van up the schoolyard. One day, two boys dropped the custard container. It fell on its side, its lid rolled off, and a yellow stream trickled down the elevated, sloping tarmac playground, through the metal railings, and out on to Church Street. Treacle pudding without custard that day, and a caning for two unlucky porters. The railings had spiked tops; just one child impaled thereon in our time.

Going errands was another almost daily requirement (no fridge or freezer for us then). Light shopping mainly, and quite fun, with a genuine small bakery, newsagent, sweet shop, two chip shops, post office, barber and greengrocer all within seven minutes of us. A

Still "steam daft", even on holiday. Twins Robert (right) and William Wilson pictured at the world famous Romney, Hythe and Dymchurch Railway in Kent. "We were Bobby and Billy in those days," said Robert.

longer trip was fortnightly, pushing an old pram overloaded with salvaged newspapers to Babes' on Upper Dale Road, some way past 'the Cavo': the Cavendish, our local retail paradise.

"Some services came to us. The cry of an itinerant rag and bone man was commonplace, and bread, milk and eggs were delivered daily, courtesy of the Co-op's horse and cart. The coalman called too, on request, as did Billy Salt, the chimney sweep.

"Public transport fascinated us. Derby's was variegated with Derby Corporation, Trent, Barton, Blue Bus and Felix to the fore. In the holidays or on Saturday mornings, Bill and I would sometimes walk into town, dallying first at 'the Cavo' in the hope of seeing a trolley bus de-wire spectacularly, thereafter taking a short cut down the decrepit alleyways of Eagle Street from The Spot to the Morledge to watch buses at work, before playing 'dares' on the old wooden footbridge – actually the towpath of the Derby Canal – across the Derwent, with its many missing floor planks, and thence to a railway bridge just north of Midland Station, a veritable Mecca for young train spotters looking to 'cop' (see for the first time) some loco rarity or other. Locos roared and belched thrillingly as they set off northwards, or rocked and clattered over pointwork as they coasted in from the north to their designated platform. Such camaraderie between lads down there, gathered in their dozens from every walk of life to enjoy the sensuous excitement of steam power.

"Our two main fun palaces were even closer to hand. Normanton Recreation Ground ('the Rec') on Warwick Avenue was under a mile away: acres of grass on which to play football or cricket according to season. Having carefully inserted the bladder into our stitched leather football and painstakingly done the lacing and inflating, we'd set off full of optimism that this would be the day when we finally managed to kick the heavy, rapidly waterlogged brute more than a few feet. Coats for goals, of course, and eventually anything up to 20 a side as onlooking lads' pleas to "Gi' us a game," were responded to sympathetically.

Derby's town centre skyline was a mass of trolley-bus wires, like these at the bottom of St Peter's Street. The Wilson twins loved to see a bus de-wire.

"The other heaven was even closer. Our garden backed on to allotments run by a local association. Adjoining them to the south were 'the Seven Fields': collectively a maze of tracks, hedgerows, trees, ditches, ponds; a wondrous surviving rural enclave. The allotments remain, but are now gated and barred to deter thieves and vandals. Those seven fields have largely succumbed to housing.

This haven for birds, frogs, newts, sticklebacks, rabbits etc was a cheap, safe, carefree exploration play area for us. It was also where our elder brother, Murray, flew his model aeroplanes, and let us go along to watch excitedly. Or he'd take us with him further afield to Rykneld pond to sail his 'pre-owned' model yacht.

"Two other haunts were a bus ride away. An hourly bus service ran round the then incomplete ring road, from Raynesway to Duffield Road, Broadway, and back. This put both Markeaton Park and Darley Park within reach, Markeaton for walks, boating and miniature train rides, and Darley Park for exploration in summer and exciting sledging in winter.

"Immediate post-war Derby was vibrant and varied. To be alive then was indeed close to bliss, and to be young and free almost heavenly."

Abingdon Street to Royce's, via the Co-op Bakery

IN THE summer of 2013 I finally met Reg Collis. The former Derbeian had been a regular correspondent through email from his home in Brisbane. But now Reg was visiting his hometown. We spent some jolly Friday lunchtimes at the White Swan in Littleover. I persuaded him to contribute to this book:

"I WAS born in August 1944, the youngest of three boys – my brothers were aged six and four years old respectively – and I grew up in Abingdon Street. Looking back now, it was a hard life for Mum and Dad, mainly for Mum because looking after a family of five was a full-time job, and she didn't enjoy any labour-saving gadgets, things like a washing machine and a vacuum cleaner. We didn't have a bathroom, and the lavatory was outside. We had to attend Reginald Street public baths for our ablutions, otherwise it was the old tub or over the sink. We had no hot running water. We just used the gas range or the open fire to heat water. We knew no different, of course, because most of our neighbours shared similar living standards.

"Abingdon Street was on the route of the Derby Carnival, and also the Rolls-Royce children's party: along Osmaston Road and up Abingdon Street to Osmaston Park and the Rolls-Royce Welfare. The carnival was really good, the floats all decorated with people dressed up. The bands included the Derby Serenaders, Regalia, and the Midshipmen. There were others, but I can't remember them after all these years

Dad spent all his working life at Rolls-Royce, and for many years he could walk there and back and enjoy his midday meal at home because we weren't far from Royce's Hawthorn Street gate. But then they moved his department to Sinfin.

"In those days, Abingdon Street was blessed with abundant shops. On the corner of our street and Handel Street we had three shops – Woolley's, Needham's and a Co-op store that had a grocery, butcher, fishmonger and tobacconist. The Co-op had the cashier system where the money was sent on the cable, through a hole in the wall, back and forth to the individual departments.

"Mum was always there to see us off to school, and she was there to greet us when we returned, always to food on the table because Dad was a stickler for set meal times. My eldest brother did well at school and went on to Central School. My other brother attended Allenton Technical School for his last two years at school. They both went on to gain apprenticeships and continue with further education by attending Derby Technical College. As for me, well, I struggled, Mum was busier when I was growing up as there were five in the family then, so I didn't get the home schooling that my brothers did. But thanks to having a good form master in my last year at school, I achieved my best results to date. Anyway, my favourite subjects were sport and sport.

"I did a paper round for which I received 10s for six days – my first independence with my own money. I loved meeting the different people, mainly the elderly men – not much older than me now – waiting on their doorsteps. They asked for the latest cricket scores from the stop press, or the half-time scores from the football. The Perrys owned the newsagent's, but the business was rundown because they spent no money on the shop. Us delivery boys had bags that were all patched-up because Mr Perry wouldn't buy new ones. Being on Osmaston Road, they enjoyed sales of papers as the workers came out of the main gates of the Carriage and Wagon Works, and Rolls-Royce. They also enjoyed good sales at Christmas with families paying weekly towards the Christmas club in order to purchase annuals for their children.

"I didn't get a Rolls-Royce apprenticeship, but eventually I got one as a maintenance fitter at the Derby Co-op, based at the bakery on Osmaston Park Road. The bakery was rated as one of the most modern in Europe as it had installed all the latest machinery and techniques.

"I had to attend Derby Technical College and complete the City and Guilds Machine Shop Engineering courses. I found myself with some former junior school mates who'd gone on to grammar school and were now apprentices with Rolls-Royce, Carriage and Wagon Works, Loco Works and other large Derby engineering companies. It was a struggle at first. I was floundering, but I tried extra hard with the maths and workshop practices and eventually got on equal terms.

Being the young apprentice, I was handed the dirty non-glamorous jobs, I hated it. I wanted to be doing meaningful work. We had six fitters, an electrician, a plumber, a sheet metal worker, boilermen and a chief engineer whom I was told earned £20 per week, which was more than 10 times what I was earning. I hoped that one day I could earn £20 per week, although the word 'inflation' wasn't then in our vocabulary.

"A few chaps used to gamble on the horses, and I was given the job of cycling to the bookies to put on a few bob for them. A chap called Tom did OK and would always give me a tip. The others just checked the winnings and said: 'Thanks.'

"There were many characters. Tim Bowers was the manager. He was responsible for increasing sales of the Co-op bread and confectionery. The output to shops around Derbyshire and Burton was enormous. He always experimented in his private kitchen to develop new products. He didn't stand fools and had a foul temper, but he would reward employees by handing them money – or ripping in half a 10s or £1 note for two to share!

I had a habit of whistling *Colonel Bogey*, and one day the manager asked the chief engineer why I did it and if it was directed at him. After that I never did it again. One fitter took snuff – yes, his nickname was Snuffy – and when I was teaching him how to light the big gas-fired ovens, I told him to look down the sight-hole. There was a blowback that burnt his eyebrow off. He had bushy eyebrows and so looked really funny with only one eyebrow. I tried hard not to laugh.

"Quite a lot of girls worked there and many relationships were formed, some eventually leading to marriage. There were also quite a few secret relationships.

"I couldn't wait to reach 21 years of age and leave. I went to Rolls-Royce at Sinfin, eventually, progressing to working between the development test beds and the pre-rigging shop. What an eye opener that was, working first on Avon turbo-prop engines, Trent, Conway and Spey, then the Spey 168 25R for the Phantom jets, the VTOL (vertical take off), then mostly on the RB211. I was fascinated by it all. The quality control was very good, the amount of paperwork accompanying each and every job had to be completed and the supervisor would finally sign-off before the engine went on to test. The pressure was on. You soon noticed the nervous foremen and supervisors, their hands

Reg Collis pictured with his two older brothers.

shaking, some aged beyond their years. Not surprisingly there seemed too many collections for funerals of some employees that were still in their prime.

"Being young and new to the job, I worked with older, experienced engineers, some of whom had been with Rolls-Royce all their working lives, never knowing anything else. They were devoted to the company, and I found this hard to understand as we were not exactly overpaid. Everyone queued up for overtime, but there was a pecking order and I was not near the top. We had three young children by then and could have done with the extra money, but the older men always got first choice and overtime often went to chaps with no family living at home.

"Then Rolls-Royce introduced a three-shifts system – mornings, afternoons and nights. Again, I didn't like them and so ended up doing regular nights as it was four nights of nine hours each, finishing on Friday at 6am and not starting back until 9pm on Monday. It seemed ideal, all that time off, but then I found I had to do the odd night's overtime to pay the bills, then two nights. I would end up feeling like a zombie and would fall asleep all too easily. Once, I dropped off on the bus and ended up in the town centre instead of at home.

But we had a good team on our night shift, which enabled some of us to catch a few hours sleep on some less busy nights. We covered for each other and it was not unknown to have the odd night off and someone would clock you in and out. That is until someone's wife phoned in and he couldn't be found, even though he was clocked on. He'd called to see a girl friend. He got the sack from Rolls-Royce – and from home.

"We had some ex RAF and Fleet Air Arm chaps join Rolls-Royce and work in our department. They were so disciplined. They'd arrive at work in their civvies clothes, change into their overalls that were pressed, they would polish their shoes or boots, they wore ties and be out on the job with military precision. Old habits die hard but it put us to shame.

"On nights everyone would nod off after eating – a warm meal and a drink, radiators on, it didn't take long to fall asleep. A lot of the chaps smoked – we hadn't been told how bad it was for us – and one chap had a pipe that he puffed away on for the entire meal break because he wouldn't get another chance until he clocked-off. He came with others from Belper in his car. One night when he'd nodded off, we shredded a little rubber into fine pieces and mixed it with his tobacco in his pouch. The next night, one of his car companions told us that, once out the gates and in the car, he'd lit his pipe. As they were driving along someone said: "Can you smell rubber?" They pulled over, all looking under the bonnet, checking the belts and hoses, and all the time he was puffing away. He told them the next day that he'd found little bits of rubber in his tobacco. He'd checked it because he could still smell rubber after he was inside his house. He questioned everyone. Trying not to crack a smile, we sympathised.

"The day shift had a foreman and supervisor as did the other shifts. They used to inter-change so as one didn't become too friendly with them. At times it came very political and we found that we couldn't book more hours up on a particular engine, so we had to book it on another one that we hadn't worked on. There were also periods when we had no work to do. We were either waiting for an engine to finish test or one to come in to be fitted out. Trying to kill time doing nothing wasn't easy. Sometimes I would go for a walk to other departments to visit a friend. On the day shift that was easier as one could catch the Rolls-Royce bus and go to another site. It's amazing how important one could look with a drawing rolled-up under one's arm.

"When the RB211 was close to reaching performance on the test beds, there were penalties looming in the contract as Lockheed required performance by due dates. If not, Rolls-Royce was penalised per day. So by 1969-1970 Royce's was close to bankruptcy and, indeed, that happened in 1971. But what an amazing engine it turned out to be.

When word got out the engine was close to reaching performances, the boffins would arrive in numbers. They would pose questions to our supervisor who asked us to explain what we are doing. The boffins didn't want to stoop so low as converse with us. We would say: "Let them ask us!" The supervisor would reply: "I daren't tell them that." One soon learned about class difference at Rolls-Royce.

"I worked my last day at Rolls-Royce in December 1970 before departing to New Zealand, then to Brisbane in 1982. But I still retain great memories of my time in Derby and the many true friends I still have there."

High Jinks at the Carriage and Wagon Works

IN THE 1950s, Ron Frost, who attended Allenton Technical School, was finding life at the Carriage and Wagon Works a laugh a minute. One of Ron's favourite stories concerned a character called Les Pickard, a crane driver on regular nights. Les, who hailed from Wirksworth, was apparently an incorrigible practical joker upon whom Ron could always count to brighten up a cold winter shift – if he was himself fortunate not to be the recipient of Les's humour.

Ron takes up the story: "One night, at his peril, Les decided to pull a prank on a fitter known to everyone as Bulldog on account of him having a face like the dog on the Churchill Insurance advertisement. Each night, after eating his 'pack up' at the 2am dinner break while sitting in the warm glow of the rivet hotter's coke fire, Bulldog had a habit of falling back into a deep sleep with his mouth wide open. It was a sight that proved irresistible to Les, who, over the years, had turned crane driving into an art form. One night, at the first sound of Bulldog snoring, he crept up into his rooftop crane, lowered the huge hook on to which he had attached a string with piece of beef fat the size of a golf ball, then proceeded to manoeuvre this towards the slumbering fitter.

"Les always boasted that he could place objects 'on to a sixpence' and with the whole shop watching with baited breath, he slowly lowered the lump of fat into Bulldog's gaping mouth without even

126

touching the sides. At the sound of loud cheering and laughter from his workmates, Bulldog awoke with a start and, seeing the crane hook and fat, together with his false teeth, disappearing into the roof of the shop, soon realised what had happened. Bulldog raged at Pickard, who was by now cowering in the crane's cab high in the roof. The air was blue and for the rest of the night there was much fist shaking in the Wirksworth crane driver's direction.

"Pickard apparently didn't come down from the crane until well into the dayshift, for fear of what the Bulldog would do to him. Thankfully, by the next night, his victim had seen the funny side of the incident and Les was reprieved. Needless to say he didn't pull any more stunts for a while. Well, not until he exploded a fog detonator under the wheels of his night shift colleague Tommy Shirtcliffe's crane at four in the morning 'just to wake him up a bit'. But that's another story."

Actually, Ron's roller coaster of fun in a Derby factory had begun almost the day after he left school. At 15 he had to report to the Carriage and Wagon Training Centre on Litchurch Lane, which was basically an extension of school where classroom theory was mixed with the practical side in the workshop.

"On one occasion we were having an examination during a maths lesson in one of the upstairs classrooms. The room was

The 1958 intake of Carriage and Wagon Works apprentices. Ron Frost is third from the right of the back row.

totally silent as all us apprentices were focussed on giving a good account of ourselves. Halfway through the exam, someone broke wind in the most spectacular and resounding fashion. The silence resumed for a few beats, then snorts of laughter and, finally, the whole class burst into paralytic and uncontrollable mirth. After a few moments, the laughter subsided and calm prevailed until the tutor, a dull, colourless man, decided that he couldn't let the matter pass without comment: 'Those boyish activities don't amuse me any more; somebody must be bad inside.'

"There was another pregnant pause of respectful silence then, by degrees, the whole room again erupted into uncontrollable laughter that went on and on and on. Realising that restoring order was now going to be impossible, the dour tutor decided to abandon the exam and angrily dismissed the class. Goodness knows what reason he gave the training school principal, Mr When, for stopping the lesson." Ron said later: "We all quoted it in cricketing terms: fart stops play."

Ron again: "Just after I came out of my time at 21, I went to work on nights with a man with the nickname of Yogi. He was a small, thin man with long, lank hair and he wore NHS spectacles with very thick lenses. Yogi was a smashing bloke and very fond of his ale. He spent a lot of his time in the Dog and Duck or fishing in the canal at Shardlow.

We made up a small night gang of two and he was the chargehand. Our task each shift was to make up two wagon under-frames, which, after completion, were lifted to the end of the shop where they were put on a set of wheels. Job done ...

"Over the months, Yogi and I became like clockwork and so expert that we were finishing our two-frame allocation, which earned us good money, by 4am. This gave us the opportunity to 'catch up on some shuteye', especially as it was summer when Yogi liked to spend most of the daytime fishing instead of sleeping. On the other side of the shop, there was permanently a line of carriages that were parked whilst the under-frames were being repaired. Yogi decided that these were just the job for a spot of kip. Climbing into them, though, proved a bit difficult because of the height. But, once there, the peace and comfort of a long upholstered compartment seat proved the ideal spot for a few hours' sleep until the dayshift arrived. Once started, we enjoyed this little perk for several nights. We always remained cautious though as being caught would have probably meant instant dismissal.

"On entering the compartment, Yogi had a habit of placing his thick-lens spectacles on the luggage rack above before going to sleep. Without them he was as blind as a bat. One morning, we were both sound asleep when I awoke with a start to the sound of hammering and the clanking of metal. On looking out of the carriage window, I realised that the dayshift had arrived and were by that time in full operation with the shop foreman striding up the shop on his round of inspection.

"Visions of getting the sack loomed and this caused me to panic. I shook Yogi, who was in another world, and shouted to him: "Wake up, we've overslept and the gaffer's coming up the bay!" I sped out of the compartment to the door, waited for my moment, and then jumped out of the carriage before slipping away unnoticed into the workforce. I then collected my things and went home purposely 'forgetting to clock-off' on my way out.

"The next night a stern-faced Yogi was waiting for me by the time-clock. "Thanks a lot mate! Where the f-----g hell did you get to? And why the f------g hell did you hide my glasses? Apparently after he woke up and I had darted off, he couldn't find his spectacles. Being almost blind without them, he said he daren't climb out of the carriage with it being so high, so he had to stay put until an inspector got on to look at the upholstery after it was lowered back on to its wheels. That was just before midday, he said.

"The inspector later found his specs and, although Yogi blamed me initially, it was obvious that they'd dropped through the mesh in the luggage rack to become wedged in the back of the seat. There was certainly no fishing for Yogi that day. After a short while we became mates again and the episode ensured that future early finishes resulted in us being content to do the newspaper crossword."

Life in the Carriage and Wagon Training School was fairly strict and getting used to working for a living was a big shock to the system. Thankfully though, as in most walks of life, there were some characters to make the days pass more quickly, as Ron again recalls:

"Sid, from Belper, was an apprentice painter and was always on the lookout to pull a prank on some unsuspecting colleague. He was a real 'Jack the Lad' and, although only small and slightly built, it never bothered him about the size of his victim. One morning, Sid decided he would pull a stunt on the biggest lad in the school, big Ross, who was also a north Derbyshire lad. Ross was a smashing lad, the proverbial gentle giant standing 6ft 2ins tall, which in 1958 was pretty tall for a 15-year-old. He was a thin, gangling lad who we nicknamed 'Snowball' on account of his mop of curly white hair.

"Each day at 9.30am we had break-time and all the apprentices assembled in the cloakroom adjacent to the workshop. The area served as a makeshift canteen and it was divided up into three aisles by thick wire mesh coat racks and bench seats. It was staffed by a kindly man we called Old Bob whose main job was caretaker and general factotum. Sid and the giant Snowball sat back to back in different aisles with only the wire mesh partition separating them. At break time, Sid bought his usual packet of Smith's crisps and, as we all know, the packet contains a small blue parcel of salt. Not fancying salt on his crisps that day, he decided that sooner than waste it, he would deposit it in someone's tea and he selected Snowball to be the recipient.

"He quickly devised a method of transporting the salt into the big lad's tea by means of his metal ruler. After carefully depositing the salt on the end of his ruler, he then slid it through the mesh before tipping into the steaming cup. With the task completed, Sid then sat back with a mischievous grin on his face waiting for Snowball to take his first sip. Snowball's reaction didn't disappoint. The loud splutter followed by expletives on his first gulp caused a large amount of suppressed laughter from the lads in Sid's aisle. Oblivious to this frivolity, the big lad recovered, got up and strode up to Old Bob at the counter who replaced the salty tea after a tasting session between the two. There was much tittering from Sid and his colleagues as Snowball sat down to continue his break.

"Flushed by his success, the next day the smirking painter decided on a repeat performance, only this time it would be even better as two onlookers had kindly donated their salt packets. Sid gleefully tipped the pile into the unsuspecting Snowball's cup and once again, the now perplexed caretaker replaced the tea. By this time Sid's mates were almost bursting trying not to be heard laughing.

"Sid was overjoyed with the success of his prank and continued it on a daily basis for the rest of the week, and each time the tea was replaced by the kindly Bob. The salty tea saga had now become the highlight of the training school's entertainment calendar and it was enhanced by the fact that Snowball was completely oblivious to it all.

"The following Monday's break couldn't come quickly enough for the lads. Snowball's aisle had now swelled in number, all covertly hoping to witness the action. The apprentice painter had become a folk hero and he fair revelled in the attention. In his wisdom, to further boost his ego, hero Sid decided to step up the entertainment, deciding that he would not only salt the big lad's first cup of tea, but also his second as well. At break-time as expected the first cup went back and, when the replacement came, it was placed dead in-line with Sid's ruler slot.

"It was perfect as Snowball then disappeared after putting the cup down. Sid quickly plopped in the first pile, then the second then, just as he was about to turn and reload, he received a tap on the shoulder and a whispered: "Here, stick these in." Turning sharply, Sid's grinning face looked upward at the tall figure before him. A hand was holding several little blue packets of salt in front of his face and suddenly, his mouth gaped open. Stood in front of him was Snowball. The game was up.

"Like a flash Snowball pulled open Sid's mouth and stuffed in all the salt including blue papers. He then held his mouth it closed for several seconds before grabbing the spluttering painter by his lapels, lifted him aloft, and then hung him on a coat peg where he remained, to the amusement of everyone, for the rest of the break. It was sometime later that Old Bob took pity on him and helped him down. I never discovered who had put Snowball wise to Sid's antics but, over the next few weeks, Old Bob always gave Sid a wry smile as he was serving him his morning tea. One thing was for sure! Sid was never spotted buying crisps again.

"Like most schools, there is always the periodical physical altercation and the C & W Training School was no exception. The sight of hordes of apprentices in green overalls tumbling out of the doorway shouting "Fight, fight, fight", thankfully only happened once in my time there.

"On this particular occasion, the 'fight', if that's what it could be called, was between two apprentice blacksmiths named Nobby and Pargio and it took place between the bike sheds after work. No one knew what the dispute was about, but no one really cared. The general opinion was that you couldn't beat a good scrap now and then, as long as it didn't involve oneself.

"Nobby was a tough little youth who later went on to play first-team football for Derby County. I first encountered him in an inter-schools match. He was kicking anything that moved and it resulted in us having a little bout of fisticuffs. Soon afterwards, we both played football for Derby Boys and I got to know him well. He was a smashing lad and I've never forgotten how much he encouraged me when I made my debut. Pargio was in the group above mine. I didn't know much about him except that he was a big hefty lad who had all the physical and mental attributes to make a good blacksmith.

"The 'square-up' began in an alleyway between two bike sheds and battle commenced with a lot of grappling and swinging each other about, with each movement taking them closer to the ranks of parked bikes. Suddenly, with a mighty heave, the stronger Pargio hoisted Nobby off the ground and flung him into the bike shed. There was a massive crashing sound as he landed on top of a row of bikes, all of which collapsed in a spectacular domino effect.

"Pargio then raced in for the kill and pounced on his sprawling victim yelling: 'Do you give in? Do you give in?' Knowing how tough Nobby was, I knew that that would be the furthest thing from in his mind and within a short space of time, as more bikes went crashing, he was soon to be on top of Pargio, asking the same question. Interestingly, up to that point in the proceedings not one punch had been thrown from either.

"A short spate of inactivity followed until Pargio, in a quiet voice and speaking through Nobby's fingers wrapped around his face, asked, 'What are we fighting about?' There was suddenly a silence and then Nobby replied: 'Well, I don't really know.' "At that point, they tentatively released each other and stood up. The onlookers remained motionless for a few moments then, when the 'wrestlers' shook hands and draped their arms around each other as they marched back into the training school to collect their coats, they realised there would be no resumption of hostilities. Bewildered at the outcome of the battle of the blacksmiths, the crowd finally dispersed to their homes, some to the railway station, some to the bus stop and others to the bike shed to collect their bikes.

"My mate Tommo was working late that evening and he didn't see the 'fight'. He was also among the last to collect his bike before the daily long haul to Castle Donington where he lived. As he pulled his collapsed bike from the rack, he was horrified to discover that being one that had taken the full brunt of the brawling blacksmiths, like several others the front wheel of his bike was bent almost double. In all, seven bikes were rendered unridable. The unfortunate thing for Tommo was that he had no bus fare to get home.

"Luckily, three members of the teaching staff were still in the school and, after telling them of his plight, they kindly obliged with the loan to set a relieved Tommo racing off to catch his bus. The tutors were themselves making there way to the bike sheds and, as Tommo turned into Litchurch Lane, he heard the sound of loud bellowing and swearing coming from the area where the fight had taken place. He paused for a moment to listen but, as time was precious, he rushed off to the bus stop.

"The next day, when Nobby and Pargio arrived at work they were ordered to report immediately to the principal's office where they were met by three stern-faced instructors. The instructors' bikes had apparently suffered the same fate as Tommo's and that accounted for the loud swearing he heard as he raced to the bus stop. Needless to say they were not at all pleased and the apprentice blacksmiths were about to pay. The full cost of their escapade was never revealed by either youth but I believe all the bikers were compensated. It was noticed also that several weeks elapsed before Nobby and Pargio again had smiles on their faces on Friday mornings after collecting their pay packets."

Memories of the Open Market

C HRISTINE KAY (now Christine Boulton) wrote from South Africa to tell me about her days helping out in Derby's old Open Market in the Morledge. Here is her story:

"It seems as if I come from a family of self-employed business people. For many years in the 1950s and 1960s, my Dad's sister and her hubby owned the Sussex Circus Post Office, along with many other Chaddesden corner shops. No wonder I ended up as a sales assistant in the Co-op toy department.

"I think a lot of old Derby people have to thank my mum's sister, my Aunt Beattie, and my Uncle Fred, for the pots, china and glassware that they sold from the pot stall at the Derby Open Market. It went for a bargain and today is probably worth 10 times more as antiques. They sold a range of goods, from the tiniest little Wade ornaments to the best cut-glass and Regency china. Many of these will have been passed down through the families, each probably having a story or memories attached to them.

"Uncle Fred was the only son of the Vicar of Chaddesden. He must have met my Aunt Beattie in his young days. It's a shame that we have no records of them, as they never had children. I think they got married in during the war. On the only photograph of them that I found, they looked dressed up for a wedding, although not in the traditional gear.

"In the 1960s – and maybe as early as the 1950s – my Aunt Beattie with my Mum and their sister in-law ran the two stalls next to the curtain stall on the outside of the Open Market, facing the

River Gardens, whereas the stalls that sold cheap, cracked pots were along the side backing on to the old Bus Station.

"My Mum would wake me up at some ungodly hour. In winter I'd dress in extra socks and sometimes two pairs of leggings, a scarf etc. My gloves had to be knitted without fingers so we could work better. It was freezing standing at the bus stop and then standing all day. Even with all that protection, my toes would still feel as though they were dropping off. But even on the cold days I would be hanging around to get my pound pocket money for helping.

"Under the counters there were two large tea crates and a wooden chest. We had to unpack all the tea, dinner and fish plates, cups, saucers, teapots, and so on. Everything had to be dusted and set out. We had a black marker-pen to write the price of 3d, 5d, 11d a plate. I learnt very quickly to add up in my head: six plates at 11d was 6 x 12 is 6 bob take off 6d – easy: 5s 6d!

"Uncle Fred would come along in his van with the best china and glassware, the boxed sets of glasses and vases, all the ornaments, dishes, the full sets of china tea and dinner services, I really liked the two and three-tier cake plates. It was all new stock collected in the week from the Stoke potteries, although a good stock was also kept in his garage storeroom at the top of his garden on Kedleston Road.

"My main job was to run up to the tea and sandwich stall and collect the tea for my two aunts and Mum and me in a huge six-cup teapot. The first drink, though, was coffee from the flask that Aunt Beattie brought with her. It had a 'drop of something' in to keep out the cold. I would then do the rounds of the other stalls, shopping for fruit and veggies for the weekend for everyone. At lunchtime off I went for the portions of fish, chips and mushy peas from across the road. I suppose a lot of the business was to the other market people for their mugs, cups. The sweet-stall lady became a good friend of mine as most of my pocket money went to her stall. Dolly Mixtures and Sherbet Fizzes come to mind.

"The summer season was good as all the visitors came down to Derby with the strange accents, perhaps here for a wedding and buying presents to take back up north or down south. We called every one "my duck" or "love" and had a lot of people return, asking for an order of an odd saucer, cup or teapot lid to replace the broken ones. They even came from Scotland with their Scottish pound notes.

"Uncle Fred also had a stall in the Market Hall. Like all the other stalls he was open every weekday except Wednesday when off he went to stock up at the Potteries. His Market Hall stall sold a lot of the better tea sets, the china animals and cut-glass vases, sets of glasses in boxes, serving dishes, etc. One of my jobs was to run along to his stall, shopping in the Market Hall on my way for the joints of meat, boiled ham and so on, for Mum and the aunts, and maybe collect a tea service or set of glasses from Uncle Fred if our stock on the Open Market was going well. He had a lot of humour and could chant and spin the tea sets like the other guys on the cheap pot side. We were taught to ring the cups against each other to check if they were sound and not cracked. Cheap cups and plates were always wrapped in newspaper but the better stock on the inside stall side was wrapped in tissue.

"It's no wonder I am such a hoarder of antique glasses, plates and ornaments. Me and my cousins all did well for our own engagement and wedding presents with each having a china tea set and dinner service given to us which we still use to this day. Happy memories. Even of that cold weather …

Memories of Tennyson Street

TED HARRISON recalls his childhood in Tennyson Street: "I must have been around four when I recall hearing the 'bull' go off to herald the commencement of the dinner hour at the Carriage and Wagon, now somewhat grandly named Bombardier. I'd run to the wooden gate of our council house in Tennyson Street and watch the Royce's workers cycling down the street, for their lunch period was of a similar length. I frequently said hello to a blind man and his helper who led him down the street every day and even at that early age I wondered what job he could have done with such a handicap. The noise of the 'bull' was similar to that made by a modern cruise ship leaving port, and would have my mother scurrying round so that our dinners were being placed on the table promptly as my dad walked in the door.

It took 12 minutes each way for him to walk to and from work, so he had 36 minutes to eat a hot dinner followed by a stodgy pudding such as spotted dick. These desserts were vital to satisfy the workingman's appetite as meat was still on ration. 'What's for pudding, Mam?' I'd gleefully yell, knowing that there would be none if I had failed to eat my greens. I'd also run to the gate if I heard the rag-and-bone man announcing out his presence by bawling: 'Ragabone, Ragabone.' He'd offer a few coppers for scrap, including old clothing, especially if made of wool. Some days his horse would deposit a steaming heap of ginger dung on the road, and the race was on to recover it and use it as fertiliser on your rhubarb or vegetable patch. It never remained on the road for long, that's for sure.

"It must have been around this time when I saw a black man for the first time. This was nothing to do with skin pigmentation. He was the coalman puffing and panting down our path with a hundredweight bag of coal slung on his back. His blue eyes suggested that he was of Anglo-Saxon descent, but every square inch of visible skin was black with accumulated coal dust. One of today's health and safety officers would have had a heart attack as a hundredweight actually weighs 112lbs, and taking turns with his equally black partner he would carry around 12 bags from his lorry on each delivery. In common with every other housewife in the street, my mother would count each bag as it was tipped into the coalhouse, with a shower of sooty dust rising each time. It would appear that nobody trusted the coalmen and, years later, I found out that this was with just cause when I met one who had recently retired. Although the housewives were counting the bags, the dodge was to have previously taken a few lumps of coal out of each and create a couple of bags extra for every lorry load. These were sold for cash to friends at a discount, or ended up in the coalmen's own coalhouses. The company owners knew nothing of this scam and I sympathise with these poorly paid delivery men who must have been exhausted at the end of each day. Try lifting 112lbs (that's over 50kg), and carrying it on your back for perhaps 20 yards, and then repeating the exercise it at least 50 times, remembering that any piece of luggage more than 20kg gets labelled as 'heavy' at today's airport and a case over 30kg is rejected at the check-in.

"Like many of the neighbours in identical houses we chose to live in a kitchen 12 feet square, despite the fact that there was a front room of much larger proportions used only at Christmas or for special occasions if we had visitors for tea. The smaller room contained the only washbasin in the house, referred to as 'the sink' and used for washing pots, faces, hair and anything else, because the bathroom contained just a cast-iron bath. The lavatory was outside and in the winter months a small paraffin lamp was used to stop the pipes freezing. The Queen apparently still uses the word 'lavatory', although doubtless she has not experienced the discomfort of having to sit there on a cold day with squares of the *Daily Herald* to read prior to committing them to their final act before they were flushed away after you had tugged on a chain dangling above your head.

"Possibly we lived in the kitchen to avoid the cost of heating two rooms. Mam would get up at 6.30am and light a fire. In the winter months I'd leap out of bed and, ignoring the ice on the inside of the bedroom windows, I'd dress in 10 seconds flat and race downstairs to huddle by the now roaring fire. Sitting there I'd make toast for breakfast by holding the bread close to the flames with a purpose-made toasting fork, cursing when a slice of bread slipped off into the fire. The kitchen had a small table against one wall with three chairs and there were two armchairs crammed into this tiny room, which also has a gas cooker. We had no TV set and during the evening Dad liked to listen to 'the wireless', whilst polluting the air with the smoke from his Will's Woodbines. There were no health warnings in those days.

"I was born on 17 March – St Patrick's Day – 1946; clearly a mistake as my sister, Mavis, was by now 13 and a pupil at Parkfield Cedars School. I was christened Edmund, although from day one I was called Teddy and later just Ted. My dad's sister, Doreen (always pronounced 'Dreen'), had married a Canadian airman with the same name during the war and he was killed in a bomber over Italy, so I was named after him. Aunt Doreen went off to Canada to meet her late husband's in-laws, remarried, and stayed there for good. I hated being called Edmund and still do. Born the same day in the next bed at the City Hospital was Jimmy Dickenson who lived in Glossop Street and was my beat friend at Nightingale infants and junior school. We were in the Cubs together, complete with waddles and tabs on our socks.

We also went to Davenport Road Methodist church and we were in the JMA (Junior Missionary Association) together. I suppose that I slipped by the wayside at some point, but Jimmy went on to become the vicar at St Edmund's Church in Shelton Lock and christened both of my daughters. Although a caring vicar he liked pop music and greyhound racing and, dare I say, he had a soft spot for the ladies that might have been the reason for him leaving the cloth and becoming a teacher. Not that you need to be a teacher to be fond of the ladies, trust me.

"In the early 1950s there was no need to lock your back door, and neighbours often had gaps in the hedges of their back gardens to allow quick access. Next to us was elderly Mrs Hayward who, during the war, had famously allowed her false teeth to fall in a jug of steaming coffee. Apparently, during an air raid she was in our half-buried Anderson shelter with my parents, my sister and another family who shared it. My dad had braved the Luftwaffe and had gone into the house to make a jug of coffee. On his return, Mrs Hayward bent over it to take in the delicious aromas when out popped her teeth and splashed into the coffee, where they quickly sank. With the special spirit in those days everyone laughed out loud and off went dad to make another supply of coffee.

Fifteen-year-old Ted Harrison (left) pictured with pals Jackie Goddard and Chris Dowson on a Henry Cavendish School holiday to Bad Aussee in Austria, circa 1961.

"At every other house lived a family with kids around my age, so street games such as snobs, marbles, hopscotch and hot rice were plentiful. The lamppost by our house was acknowledged as the official lurky post for games such as hide and seek, where a safe haven was required. Shouting: "Lurky, lurky 123" at the top of your voice guaranteed sanctuary. Mr Stone had a son and three daughters and lived opposite some set-back garages, and this area was the acknowledged street football pitch. Each evening, as the game commenced, he would appear at his gate and tell us to 'bugger off somewhere else'. The street lawyer, Johnny Smith, would tell him that we were on public land and he had no legal right to ask us to leave, or words to that effect, as Johnny's dad could outswear anybody in the street and his numerous offspring had an amazing vocabulary for these situations. Mr Stone could then be seen peering from behind his curtains waiting for the ball to go over the miniature hedge into his tiny front garden, no more than 6ft from his house. The unfortunate kid who touched the ball last was expected to hop the small hedge and retrieve it before Mr Stone could confiscate it whilst screaming a shower of swearwords. On occasions, sensing that he didn't have enough time to get to his front door, he would leap out of the window to intercept the unfortunate child and deliver a considerable smack around his nearest ear. Two things here – if you didn't jump into his garden the other kids would slap you anyway, and there was no point complaining to your parents or you might be on the receiving end of another. One of the Stone kids would return the ball the following day and the sequence of events started all over again. It certainly improved our ball control and I never ever saw Mr Stone in anything but a grumpy mood. Eventually he took his family off to Tasmania and they never returned. There was a second Smith family with two pleasant and attractive daughters called Margaret and Marylyn who joined in the games but always politely declined my offer to play doctors and nurses.

"The area between Osmaston Road and Ascot Drive was known as 'The Camp' and consisted of tiny prefabricated dwellings left over, I believe, from a wartime military camp. The residents were amongst the poorest in the town and usually had loads of kids and mongrel dogs. After the Stone family emigrated, a large family who had been living on The Camp moved in. I will call them the Bloggs family and Mrs Bloggs seemed to have a baby every year whilst Mr Bloggs never had (or appeared to want) a job. With the exception of the oldest boy, the remainder were very similar nice looking kids with blond hair and blue eyes. The other was as ginger as you can get and was the cause of speculation among the neighbours. Clearly finances were an issue and when Mrs Bloggs was seen buying food (and cigarettes) from Hodnett's and paying with a stack of one-shilling coins it was clear that things were so desperate that the electricity meter had been raided. This would lead to a visit to court and a fine that plunged them further into the mire. This brings me to the rent man. Can you believe that this weedy looking middle-aged guy was loose in the street with potentially today's equivalent of £1,000 in a leather bag hanging from his shoulder? He was unarmed and untrained in self-defence but I never recall him being robbed. I think that the weekly rent was around £1 but the Bloggs family offered around 5s on a good day. I don't know in what year the rent collectors started to be robbed on a regular basis but this must have been why they eventually went the way of the dinosaurs.

"Although my dad always told me never to talk to strange men, parents in those days seemed content to rely on the fact that their kids would come in for meals or when dusk arrived. They didn't mind that we whirled winter warmers around which would terrify today's job's-worth health and safety fanatics. These devices consisted of a Lyles Golden Syrup tin pierced with holes made with a six-inch nail and attached to a loop of twine. They were filled with bits of newspaper, wood and coal before being set alight and whirled around to create a bellows effect on the blazing innards. With no TV sets, all manner of games took place and disputes were quickly settled and arguments forgotten.

Shopping

"Supermarkets hadn't arrived in England and as no one had a car the area was reliant on a variety of small shops. Opposite our house was a cobbler's ran by Mr Calladine who was deaf and dumb. When you went into his shop you had to wait until he glanced at one of several mirrors to see that he had a customer. Sometimes you needed to attract his attention and on a windy day this could be achieved by opening and closing the shop door so that he might feel the draught. Another way was to jump up and down as if on an invisible pogo stick so that he might feel the vibrations. For me a few years later, he would fit new cogs in my football boots as the nails had probably come through the soles and would be hurting my feet. It was necessary to show your mother the small bleeding holes before she would pod out for the new cogs, and you would need to wait until Friday when dad got paid. The football boots had hard toecaps and it was hard to 'Bend it like Beckham'. It was much easier in fact to boot the ball high over the bar. Perhaps though, Mr Beckham wouldn't have broken his metatarsal with his foot comfortably fitted into one of my well-dubbined boots. There was also a herbalist on the main Osmaston Road and looking back I can understand why he had the most miserable of faces as it can hardly have made much of a living for him. Much more cheerful was Mr Wathall at the tiny grocer's shop next door where my mother would tear off a small voucher from her ration book and buy me 2oz of pear drops.

"Mrs Hodnett ran the nearest shop, and her grandson, Kenny Lucas, was one of my best friends and still is to this day. Ken's dad, Harry, ran a small greengrocery outlet from an attached garage but he chain-smoked Capstan Full Strength and didn't reach old age. Mrs Hodnett worked six and a half days every week and was 81 before she retired, when an Asian family took over. She was one of the first retailers in the late 1950s to offer frozen Jubblys to the local kids at a cost of 4d. It was best to make yourself scarce if you saw Lenny Smith sucking one. When all the goodness had gone he would be looking for someone to hurl the cricket ball-sized block of ice at or, worse still, if he could catch you he would stick it down your shirt. As a child I had great fleet of foot and I owed this almost entirely to Lenny. I can remember an American soldier regularly walking down the street to meet a young lady at the top end, and the Smith siblings must have heard their dad's comment of 'over-sexed, overpaid and over here', for they barracked him unmercifully every time he stoically walked by, showing no sign of having heard. I was secretly impressed by his indifference.

"Nearly opposite Mrs Hodnett's shop lived a woman named Molly. She was normally pleasant and well behaved but when the moon was full (or new – I am not sure which) she went spectacularly off the rails and would be dragged off to the asylum for a few days. As the houses had no inside toilets, chamber pots were common and on one occasion Molly leaned out of the bedroom window and threw the contents of one over the postman. The story quickly spread and whilst I'm sure that sympathies were with the poor postman, there was much sniggering and exaggeration of the tale. That's when I learnt about lunatics and since then I have met hundreds of them and frequently been described as such myself.

"The main shopping would be done at the Co-op and there were numerous of them scattered about Derby. We used the one on Ascot Drive that was on The Camp. Most survivors of the era will be able to tell you their mum's Co-op cheque number. Ours was 54096 and every few months the Co-op paid a dividend based on what you'd spent, and known colloquially as 'The Divi'. This was indeed a red-letter day and the two or three pounds handed back would in part be used on a small treat.

Nightingale School

"In truth I can't remember too much about the Nightingale Infant and Junior schools. I recall that the toilet block was 50 yards across the playground and had no roof, so the kids quickly learnt not to get caught short on a rainy day. There were chalk lines above the urinals claiming various records but we will not delve into that here. Let's just say that it was a bad idea to be playing 'fag cards' on the other side of the wall. Young boys are often quite cruel by nature and I was grateful not to be fat or, worse still, ginger. We had one of each variety in our class and their lives were generally made a misery. On occasions, and unexpectedly, your mother might grab you by the scruff of the neck and thrust your head into a bowl of hot water. Oblivious to your screams she would then proceed to scrub your head violently with carbolic soap. This could only mean one thing – the Nit Nurse was due to visit the school on the following day. The Nit Nurse would sieve through your hair with a fine-toothed comb looking for an infestation. On one occasion a single unfortunate soul tested positive, and after being shorn of his curly locks his scalp was painted with a purple coloured compound called Gentian Violet to flush out and exterminate any of the more determined nits that were in hiding. When back in class, the teacher cautioned everyone not to tease or laugh at the unfortunate wretch, but when the traumatised lad came sulking into the classroom mass hysteria broke out, compounding his worst fears. The teacher, herself fighting back the urge to join in, grabbed the nearest boy and rapped his knuckles hard with a 12in ruler, an act that reinstated some kind of calm. Needing to find a scapegoat, at least she picked on a serial misbehaver who was hardened to this form of punishment and had recently been moved from the back of the class to the front, where his behaviour could be more closely monitored. Looking around the class I noticed that the ginger lad looked extremely happy, knowing the pressure was off him for a few days. Gentian Violet was applied to the heads and faces of children for a variety of reasons, and any kid with his mouth liberally coated with the stuff was always last to be offered a swig from the pop bottle when it was passed around.

"The most feared event of every child in the school was a visit to the Mill Hill Clinic dentist. The initial examination took place in school and gave no clues of the terrors waiting at Mill Hill. Kids needing dental treatment were issued with a card to take – white if you required a filling, green if a tooth needed removing. On entering the waiting room you were greeted by a small line of trembling boys and girls who looked like they had just seen their first ghost. From long and bitter experience the staff had made escape almost impossible so whilst the natural inclination was to run for your life, you had little choice but to sit down. It was then that you would hear screams coming from behind the surgery door accompanied by the low frequency sound of the drills used in those days, and you would immediately adopt the same complexion as the others. The trembling became worse as the lad in front of you was manhandled into the surgery and the screaming commenced again. When your turn came you were plonked into a huge rubbery looking chair and if you screamed during the initial non-too-gentle examination, a gas mask was clamped on your face. This is where the most screaming took place as the dentist grappled with you to keep it in position, and the experienced dentist did this from behind so the flailing toecaps of the tougher kids could not harm him. After waking up with your mouth full of cotton wool bungs, you were ushered, weeping gently, back into the waiting room where a new group of terrified kids awaited their fate. Much to the embarrassment of my mother, sister Mavis apparently leapt out of the chair during an attempted filling and made a run for it, actually managing to breach the defences, never to return. This was the only recorded escape.

"School reports were produced with inevitable comments such as 'must try harder' or 'lacks concentration'. My classic report stated: 'Whilst generally well behaved, Teddy can dream up the most amazing excuses when faced with the prospect of punishment and he should consider fiction writing as a future career." Basically it was a polite way of saying that I'd lie until my teeth fell out when the need arose. The teachers always called me Teddy rather than Edmund, and for that I was grateful. Somehow they knocked an education into me and I passed my 11-plus to go to Central School.

School Holidays and Saturdays

"Not too many of the local residents had a proper summer holiday but if your dad worked for the railway he could get free passes, so for the first five years of my life we had holidays in Great Yarmouth, and then further afield such as Jersey and St Ives, and once even to Menton in the South of France when I was nine. I've no idea how my dad could afford it as my mother never worked. During the main summer holiday we made dens and brewed Camp coffee by adding hot water to a treacle-like substance in an HP Sauce-style bottle. We drank so much that everything we ate tasted of it until we eventually got banned. We played endless games of Monopoly and one marathon game was so even that the bank ran out of money. We left the game set up in someone's shed and wrote to Waddington's, using a John Bull Printing Outfit No 2. They actually replied fairly quickly and told us to issue IOU's.

"On Saturdays throughout the year, all those with sixpence to spare went to the 'tanner rush', which was a presentation of several children's films at the Broadway cinema in Allenton centre (later a Fine Fare and more recently a Somerfields supermarket). There were morning and afternoon matinees and the cost was 6d in the stalls or 9d for the posh kids in the circle or balcony. Here we would marvel as Buster Crabbe played Flash Gordon as he conquered the universe in a space ship, which seemingly travelled around in circles at around 5mph, spluttering and crackling with sparks like a malfunctioning Roman candle on Bonfire Night. There was always a cliff-hanger finish where the evil Emperor Ming was about to finish off our hero, Flash, and it was guaranteed to bring you back the following Saturday. There would also be a Looney Tunes cartoon such as Bugs Bunny or The Road Runner and a short comedy featuring the likes of The Three Stooges or Laurel and Hardy. There would be a 10-minute interval when the house lights came on to reveal a lady walking down the isle with a tray of orange 'suckers' costing 3d each, and fighting to stay on her feet as a rush of kids tried unsuccessfully to form an orderly queue. The occasional ice-lolly, which was always called a sucker, had a star stamped on the wrapper entitling the lucky owner to a free cinema ticket. Finally the main feature would usually be a Western such as Hopalong Cassidy or The Cisco Kid, who had the most unlikely of partners called Pancho. It was a fantastic experience and something you looked forward to all week.

"At the age of 11, I was taken to the Baseball Ground by a friend and paid 9d to stand in the 'Boys' Pen' to watch Derby County playing in the Third Division North. I was hooked for life after the first game and the team were promoted the same season.

"The 1950s moved along quickly and I remember getting a Coronation Mug in 1953. By 1954 rationing had finally finished and in 1955 the first car appeared in our street, a Morris Minor proudly owned by Georgie Sharp's dad who came originally from Paisley and was incomprehensible. By 1957 I was allowed trips to Tamworth or even Crewe for the purposes of train-spotting and the hairs would stand up on your back when an express train belching smoke and steam hurtled through Tamworth Low Level station at 100mph en route from one of the northern cities to London Kings Cross. At Crewe, the braver lads would 'bunk the sheds' which meant running over the railway lines to the engine sheds in the hope of spotting a locomotive whose number was not yet crossed off in their Ian Allen train-spotter's book. This risky venture usually ended when a railwayman spotted the offenders and yelled that he was fetching the police. Around 1956 my grandparents, who lived in Grosvenor Street, had a black and white television installed. It was the size of a jukebox with a tiny 9-inch screen and along with aunts, uncles and cousins we used to go and watch it on a Saturday night. I remember the famous Potter's Wheel interlude where someone modelled clay on a spinning wheel for 15 minutes as a natural break between programmes. We had our first television set in 1958, a 12-inch model that received only the BBC.

Central School for Boys

"In 1957 I set off to my new school which was housed in the old mansion house at the top end of Darley Park; a most wonderful setting. This meant catching a trolley bus to the Market Place, and if you were lucky the two trolley poles which connected with the overhead lines would come adrift and fly all over the place, often wreaking devastation on other overhead wires in the vicinity. The conductor would slide out a long bamboo pole with a hook on the end and struggle to catch the special loops on the trolley poles before restoring power to the bus. This was not an easy task and passengers shouted encouragement that kept everyone amused.

"At the Central School for Boys the culture of fagging was long established, and the previous year's intake was intent of wreaking vengeance on the smartly dressed new bunch. This involved ages old traditions such as being thrown over 'The Wall', which was only 1ft high on one side but 6ft on the other. It was mandatory to have your cap removed and thrown in the holly bushes, and quite often you would follow it without warning. The falling of snow (quite common in those days) would provide amusement for all except the poor fag encased in a huge snowball hurtling down the hill and gaining in size so that only hands head and feet would be showing before it crashed into the balustrade on the bank of the River Derwent, narrowly saving the victim from drowning. We used to cross the river to play football on Darley Playing Fields, although just beyond the old tearooms was another field that, for obvious reasons, was called the Cow Patch. We changed first at the school and there were no showers or washing facilities. After the game you had to dress in your school clothes, with limbs covered in mud and bovine excrement, and make your way home to meet the wrath of your mother.

"After the first year the entire school was relocated to Breadsall Hilltop and was renamed Sir Henry Cavendish School. Much to our initial horror and later delight, girls were introduced to the school. The old customs gradually died out and somehow they knocked an education into us. The know-it-all reformists scrapped grammar schools a few years later and the school was taken over by feral youths who reduced the morale of dedicated teachers to virtually zero. What was a brand new state of the art building in 1958 was in the main demolished a little over 40 years later. Some pupils hated school and others, like me, really enjoyed it. Not at all for the lessons but more for the sport and general good time that we had. The end-of-term reports became very poetic, especially from one particular teacher: 'Your son sets low personal standards and then consistently fails to achieve them,' or 'Since my last report your child has hit rock bottom and started to dig.'

"Some left at 15, which was the earliest you could go and when jobs and apprenticeships were plentiful. I chose to stay an extra year to retake the 'O' Levels that I'd failed the first time through laziness. We formed a football team called Brunswick Rangers and it lasted for 22 years with several founder members still playing at the time of the final game. Again with lots of choice, I opted to join the Signal and Telecommunications Department of British Rail in Nelson Street, because it paid £7 per week against the £5 offered by Rolls-Royce for an engineering apprenticeship. This would be in 1963, memorable for its severe winter. We still had no telephone but the postal service was so good that I could send a postcard to my mother at 9am and it would arrive in time to tell her that I wouldn't not be cycling home for my dinner (we still had our main hot meal at lunchtime). This might happen if work asked me to hop on a train to deliver or collect an important item and I sent these cards regularly without a single one failing to be delivered by the 'second post'. They had two deliveries on weekdays in those days and even one delivery on Christmas Day. How things have changed. I left Tennyson Street in 1970 to get married and the same group of residents were still there in the same houses. I missed them all, but at least I no longer had to traipse outside during a hailstorm to the lavatory."

Memories of Horton Street

G ROWING UP in Horton Street, just off Osmaston Road, during the 1950s and 1960s might not have been the ideal place one would have chosen, but it had its compensations with events and characters that are remembered to this day. That is the view of Colin Boulton, born in Derby in 1946 and today retired and living in Johannesburg, South Africa.

"I've memories of going to St James's Church Infants School from about 1952 to 1957. The school was at the top of Douglas Street and Dairyhouse Road, and that was in the days when a non-white face was something of a rarity. So how excited everyone was when a young Yugoslav kid joined the school. The highlight at playtime was to get him to speak in English. It was fascinating to hear a foreign accent.

"I particularly remember two of the teachers we had at St James's. My favourite was a man called Pat Connor who, among other roles, had the unfortunate task of being the school football coach. As I'd shown a bit of a flair for being able to stop people in their tracks during playtime, I was identified as an appropriate candidate for the vacant centre-half position in the school football team. Pat Connor really was a memorable man and had the patience of Job, he used to give bus tokens to each of the team and we'd be off on a 33 bus to the Cavendish from where we would walk to Normanton Rec for an hour of intensive training.

"Mr Connor knew what he was talking about when he trained us – or so it seemed at the time – and I always remembered him showing us that if the opponents' left-winger was attacking us, then our defence had to be lined up at a 30-degree 'slope', with our right-back the most forward player, ready to tackle their left-winger. The theory was that if the left-winger beat our right-back, then our centre-half would glide across to tackle him. In the unlikely event of the left-winger beating the centre-half (me) it still left us with a left-back handily placed to also glide across and dispose of the left-winger in the best means deemed appropriate at the time and taking into account the importance of the match. I use the words 'dispose of' purposely as our left-back at the time was a lad called Dave Sabine, who, to put it politely, was a little overweight and had a tendency to mistime tackles so it was quite a normal sight to see the ball, the left-winger and Dave Sabine land together over the touchline in a big heap.

"We must have been doing something right at training because we reached a cup final of some sort and were due to play Beaufort School, from Chaddesden, at the Royal School for the Deaf ground on Ashbourne Road with a kick-off time of about 5pm. Our team was kept back at St James's School where Pat Connor provided us all with sandwiches and a bit of cake before we were piled into two cars for the journey to the game. There was a large crowd of fellow pupils and parents filling the touchlines and we were drawing 0-0 with about 10 minutes to go. Although Beaufort were favourites to win, we'd given them a real game and a half so far.

"Ten minutes from time, their right-winger, a real speedy kid called Fred Alexander, came down the right wing, past our left-back as though he wasn't there, then centred the ball as hard as he could. The crowd gasped and our defence stood rooted to the spot as the ball was caught by a gust of wind that bent the ball into the far top left-hand corner of the net, well beyond the reach of our goalie. It gave Beaufort a 1-0 victory. In later years I played football with Fred Alexander for the Rolls-Royce tool room in the R-R inter-departmental football tournament for the Claude Johnson Trophy. He often related the 'wonder goal' of which he was so proud.

"The other teacher from St James's School that I remember well was a man called Mr Herod who was better known as 'Pop' Herod. If memory serves me right he taught us 'sums' and religion. I well remember him explaining the miracle of the five fishes and two loaves – or was it five fish and five loaves? – feeding 10,000 people.

"One of my close friends at St James's Infants was a boy named David Hook whose parents owned a sweet shop on the corner of Malcolm Street and Alexander Street. Dave and I were good friends who used to meet up at his shop to walk the short distance up Malcolm Street to school each morning, and the same at home time. One day, when we were about 11, we were both given envelopes to take home to our parents. Little did we know the contents but were soon to find out as we entered his mum's shop and gave he gave her his letter. What followed was a perfect example of a mother being overwhelmed with pride, love and affection for an offspring. She screamed, she jumped, she kissed another customer, and gave sweets to other kids in the shop.

"'Our David' had passed his 11-plus and was going to go to Bemrose School in the new term. Now I was worried! I knew I wasn't as brainy as Hooky because, like most footballers, I thought studying was not half as important as throwing two coats on the ground and taking penalties for an hour after school. It was with some apprehension that I walked down Alexander Street, passed Scotties grocer's shop on the corner of Osmaston Road, and walked slowly down Horton Street to home. My Mam used to be a waitress at Pop Deesh's café at the top of Dexter Street in those days, so I had to wait until she came home before I could give her my letter. All my fears of failure disappeared when Mam announced that I'd passed my 11-plus and I was going to go to Sir Henry Cavendish Technical School in the September. This was great because it was a brand new school on Breadsall Hilltop that was going to be opened in the September. The boy next door to us, Alan Beal, already went to the school – although it was called Central School in Darley Park before becoming Sir Henry Cavendish – and what's more, it was for both boys and girls. I couldn't wait for the summer holidays to be over and school to begin.

"Having said that, the summer holidays of 1958 proved to be memorable, if only for the football that a lot of us used to play on Ivy Square from 2pm until it got too dark to continue. We took great pleasure in demonstrating our skills as the buses going to Shelton

Lock or Sinfin Lane pulled up to drop off or pick up passengers. During one game, however, I went sliding over the grass, only to come to a dead stop with a 2in piece of a beer bottle sticking out of my knee. The resulting scream must have been heard as far away as the railway station as the fright of seeing blood squirting from my knee bought the game to a sudden halt. Vic Hancock was the eldest playing that day and therefore assumed control of the situation. Fortunately, he lived in the bottom corner of Ivy Square and he lifted me up and carried me over to the surrounding fence and shouted his mam to come out. Mrs Hancock was a star. She was more like 'one of the boys' and always reminded me of Olive Oyl from the Popeye cartoon. She never ever grassed on us to our parents, no matter what we'd been up to. On this afternoon she carried me over to her house, sat me on a chair outside the back door and proceeded to tell me all the reassuring stories that an 11-year-old who was expecting his leg to be amputated wanted to hear. She washed my knee, pulled out the glass (I've still got the scars to this day) put some Savlon or TCP or something on my knee, bandaged it all up nicely and gave me a tanner to stop crying.

"The summer holidays soon passed by and in the meantime Mam had kitted me out with the new school uniform for Sir Henry Cavendish. As it was a brand-new school, and I was part of the very first intake, parents and pupils went there for an introduction prior to actually starting the school. It was amazing. Everything was new and gleaming. We were told where our individual lockers were situated and because it was a new school we were told that we had to wear 'slippers' for walking around the school so the wooden floors wouldn't get scuffed from leather soles! Excitement and enthusiasm were the key words for everyone.

"Day One at Sir Henry Cavendish finally arrived. I must have been awake at 4am and was ready with new school uniform, new satchel, new cap, new pencils, shiny clean face and a really neat haircut ready to proudly walk to Ivy Square on Osmaston Road to catch either the 66 bus from Shelton Lock into town or the 88 from Sinfin Lane into town. Alan Beal, the lad from next door, was already at the bus stop and I was pleased to see a familiar face that probably knew the ropes, being an older pupil of the school. We eventually arrived in the Market Place, and then made the short walk to Tenant Street where we were to catch either the Perth Street bus or the Wollaton Road bus to Breadsall Hilltop. There were hundreds of pupils in Tenant Street, all decked out in their new regalia and all carrying their slippers as instructed!

"Oh no! There was no worse a feeling in the world for a brave 11-year- old kid full of the excitement of starting big school, than realising in the very first hour of the very first day that the very first instruction given had been forgotten … my bloody slippers were still at home. A sprint across the Market Place, an almighty leap onto the steps of a 66 bus as it passed the Kardomah had me gasping for breath as I sat upstairs pondering my fate for being late on the first day. I covered the 320 yards from Ivy Square to the bottom of Horton Street in a little less than two minutes, was up the stairs into my bedroom before Mam even realised I was back. 'Forgot my slippers!' was all I yelled as I started the return journey to school. I eventually got to Sir Henry Cavendish at about 9.10am, but at least I was wearing my school slippers.

"Being one of three children with a wonderful mother who worked two or three jobs at the same time to ensure that we never went short, I soon realised that if I wanted anything 'extra' in life then I had to jolly well work for it. This started when I was about 12 and became involved in an entrepreneurial adventure based on our close proximity to the Baseball Ground. Each Saturday when the Rams were playing at home, Horton Street and the other streets surrounding the ground became filled with cars of supporters travelling into the match. There was a regular crowd of drivers who used to park in Horton Street and I soon befriended some of them as a cheeky 12-year-old who only charged a bob to 'wash and polish your car, sir?' I had a regular clientele with particularly fond memories of a farmer who always paid a bit extra if it was a cold afternoon. If I was lucky, I could finish the washing by 3.10pm and make a quick dash up Shaftsbury Street, down Shaftsbury Crescent and into the boys' enclosure for 9d before half-time. Even better was when the man on the gate would let a few of us over the railings at half-time into the Normanton Stand to sit down and enjoy the second half.

"Those were the days of Ray Straw, Ken Oliver, Jessie Pye, Tommy Powell and Jack Parry all playing for the Rams. If on occasion, I was too late to make it to the match, I would more often than not spend all my hard-earned money at Mrs Bull's corner shop at the corner of Shaftsbury Street. My favourite sweets were chocolate éclairs but I was also partial to a tin of Fussell's condensed milk which I would guard with my life until I could get it home, get the tin opener round it and then dig into it with a teaspoon until I nearly made myself sick … but I loved it.

"The money I earned from car washing was supplemented by both a morning paper round and an evening round as well. I used to deliver newspapers in the area covering Horton Street, Dexter Street, Ivy Square, Bateman Street, Douglas Street and Alexander Street. I worked for Jim Stokes, who had the newsagent's on Osmaston Road with his wife, Wendy, and sons, Robin and Paul. Jim Stokes was a really likeable man and was probably the first person in Derby to own a Mini Van when they came out in about 1959. It was a dark green van that he parked with pride in front of his shop. Brian Clough would occasionally call in at Jim's for a morning paper and always greeted people who spoke to him.

"As I grew older, the car washing on a Saturday afternoon gave way to a far more lucrative career. One of my jobs at home was to wash the front windows for Mam. But when Mrs Hodgkinson and Mrs Hicking asked me to do theirs for them as well, I realised that here was an opportunity not to be missed. I mentioned the idea to my best mate at the time, Chris Bowmer, who also went to Sir Henry Cavendish and who later became an apprentice with me at Rolls-Royce. He was all for it, so we put our plan into action.

"A new family had moved into Horton Street. They'd just returned from Australia. They were a lovely couple and they had a gorgeous blonde daughter. More importantly, they had a 15ft-long ladder, and, yes, we could borrow it as long as we washed their windows for nothing. Chris and I usually spent about five hours on a Saturday afternoon washing windows upstairs and downstairs and within about five weeks we had built up a round of about 20 houses. As well as being financially rewarding, it also gave us an education about growing up and adult life. One afternoon

I nearly fell off the ladder when I was met by the sight of one of the local housewives being, shall we say 'overfriendly', with one of our 17-year-old friends. As a 16-year-old, it must have taken me nearly 15 minutes to come cautiously down the ladder. About three months later, her husband found out what was going on when he returned home early one afternoon and must have been greeted by a similar sight. He packed his van the very same day and moved out of the house, never to be seen in Horton Street again. I must report that the woman and her young beau did eventually get married, although how long the marriage lasted is anyone's guess. Maybe the current window cleaner knows.

"Another sight was at a downstairs window when I arrived unexpectedly to wash Gerry's windows. Gerry was the oldest man in the street and had never been married. He must have been 75, if he was a day, but on the afternoon I arrived to do his windows he was being serviced like a 17-year-old on the settee by a 74-year-old female acquaintance. It was not a pretty sight and maybe it was subconsciously the reason why Chris and I gave up the round not long after and after that concentrated on our apprenticeships at Rolls–Royce. But that's another story … "

Colin Boulton (left) and Chris Bowmer just after they had finished their window cleaning round on a Saturday afternoon in 1963.

That Glorious Summer of 1959

IT WAS a glorious summer, 1959. Derbyshire sweltered in record-breaking temperatures – and we'd never heard the expression "global warming". So if you were forced to go on strike against your will, then at least you could take advantage of the weather.

As it happened, those scorching months coincided with a national printing dispute that compelled my father to come out on strike together with the rest of his colleagues at the *Derby Evening Telegraph*. It would be hard to imagine a less likely union activist than my father, but he was also a realist: had he ignored the instructions of the National Graphical Association, then he wouldn't have had a job to return to. And at least he could spend what would have been working days now watching Derbyshire play cricket.

Actually, life was difficult for those on the picket line. Strike pay was negligible, which meant that the Rippon household had to tighten its collective belt. The first thing to go was tobacco, although one Sunday evening my father caused pandemonium when he lit his pipe in the house and my mother thought the chimney was on fire. Desperate for a smoke, he'd gone mooching into the back garden, filled his pipe with dried rose leaves, then returned to puff contentedly on the result, which, of course, was a mini-bonfire. My mother's response made for an interesting accompaniment to the hymns being sung with such reverence on the Light Programme's *Sunday Half Hour*.

It was a strange year in many ways. Although January was very cold, it was the sunniest on record and every other month produced higher than average temperatures. There was that long, hot, dry summer that lasted from early May to mid-October. Even with windows wide open, locals found restful sleep a rare commodity, and working in the factories, mills and foundries in particular became highly unpleasant – unless you were on strike, of course. For children, the long summer meant plenty of opportunities to enjoy the county's parks and to play in the streets. I was 14 and it is a year that has always stuck in my mind.

But what else was going on locally in 1959? Well, one of Derby's best-loved adopted sons, Philip Noel-Baker – one of the town's MPs for more than 20 years – was awarded the Nobel Peace Prize for a lifetime's work promoting peace and disarmament, work during the Russian Famine in the late 1920s and with refugees during the Second World War.

In May the *Evening Telegraph* published a feature by one of its regular columnists, "Albert Street", who asked: "Has Derby a Colour Bar?" As new immigrants had begun arriving from the Commonwealth, there had been much talk of non-white school leavers finding it difficult to obtain suitable work in the town because employers were selecting white workers ahead of them, regardless of qualification or ability. As the columnist pointed out, it would be hard to prove this was the case since: "No firm will admit publicly … that the colour of an apprentice's skin could affect his chances of securing an apprenticeship."

He also suggested that fear of an unfavourable reaction from existing workers might put employers off taking on immigrant workers. The previous year, factory workers at Milford had gone on strike when a Punjabi was given work there. The strikers had claimed that the management had agreed not to take on "coloured" workers when white workers were available. Albert Street was horrified to relate that, although the two sides had eventually reached an agreement, this had occurred only after the Punjabi had been dismissed. The columnist believed the "traditional insularity of the British" and a general mistrust and dislike of anything visibly non-British was to blame. "It may be fair to argue that when in Britain you should do as the British do, although heaven knows why you should, provided you are not breaking any laws." Despite his concerns

Albert Street was convinced that there was very little disharmony in the town: "Derby strikes me as an admirable example to many towns in the way that it accepts our guests from other lands."

In late June, that national printing dispute erupted. While national newspapers were unaffected, work at all regional newspapers, including the *Evening Telegraph,* and at printing works like Bemrose's in Litchurch, was brought to a halt. Throughout the six-week strike, non-union workers at the *Evening Telegraph* produced a small "emergency bulletin" for its readers. Initially, this took the form of a four-page typewritten publication, but later evolved into a small printed edition. Eventually the print and paper workers became the first manual workers to secure a 40-hour working week.

In case the fine English weather had not satisfied Derbyshire folk, international air travel was now on offer. Under the tagline: "Fly Derby and meet the sun!" Derby Airways – the forerunner of BMI – advertised flights to Dublin, Guernsey, Jersey and the more exotic climes of Ostend, Luxembourg and Corsica. The airline operated out of Derby Airport at Burnaston, which had been opened in 1937 and for much of the Second World War had served as a flight-training centre for the RAF.

Another advertisement, this time for Derby travel agents, Briggs and Hill, in St Peter's Street, offered a "wonderful holiday in Jersey" with return flights from Derby, full board hotel accommodation, "wonderful full-day and half-day excursions", the services of a holiday rep, free baggage insurance and a "guarantee of a full refund in case of illness". All of this cost just £19 5s. Unfortunately, the advertisement neglected to mention the length of the holiday.

If Derbeians preferred to spend their hard-earned wages on something more tangible in 1959, there were plenty of advertisements from local businesses to investigate. Telefusion of London Road offered "unbeatable all-in rental terms" for a range of televisions, including the new Murphy 17in tabletop set. Alex Owen Ltd on London Road was promoting a new Jackson refrigerator for 35 guineas. Alternatively, the same appliance could be bought on hire-purchase with a deposit of £7 10s followed by 104 weekly payments of 6s 2d. The attraction of immediately acquiring a gleaming new fridge that could, for an additional charge, be supplied with legs, might well have encouraged many a house-proud Derbeian to part with an extra ten per cent.

Other advertisements catered to mothers keen to give their sons "pride in their appearance", like that placed by Strand Boys' Clothiers & Outfitters who could supply suits, sports coats, rainwear, blazers, pullovers and even jeans. "Your boys," the advertisement reminded mothers, "deserve a good and reasonably priced outfit."

Perhaps the fashion-conscious Derby lady might have been tempted by the Derby Co-operative Society's promotion of Ballerina fully-fashioned nylon stockings. The "bewitching Ballerina nylons" were "the finest stockings money can buy" and featured a special "ladder stop" at top and bottom for longer-lasting wear.

In June, the *Evening Telegraph* reported a "strange object, which appeared to be hanging motionless in the sky above the Derby area". One of the first to spot the UFO was Alfred Green of Mickleover, a special constable. The following morning dozens of calls were placed by concerned Derbeians. However, a spokesman from the RAF, who identified the object as a large meteorological balloon, soon soothed fears of alien invasion, or of Soviet spies over the Rolls-Royce works.

As 1959 drew to a close, Derbeians looked forward to developments in the townscape. The first tower block of the new Derby and District College of Technology in Kedleston Road had opened, while the town's major department store, Ranby's, was preparing to move into new purpose-built premises. The store, which already had premises on Victoria Street, had acquired the 200-year-old Queen's Head pub next door. Publicans Mr and Mrs Fowler celebrated the last night of business at the end of December with a party for regulars who presented the couple with a parting gift. While there was much sadness at the closing of one of Derby's oldest inns, this was matched by the anticipation of a much-enlarged Ranby's. The new store was expected to have two acres of sales room on the ground and first floors, while the third floor was to be devoted to a large restaurant, a hair salon and other services and would take three years to complete. Westfield wasn't even a twinkle in an architect's eye.